DUBLIN

A thousand and one intriguing facts

House of Commons, Dublin

DUBLIN

A thousand and one intriguing facts

by
Gill Davies

◆ BOOK ◆ BLOCKS ◆

This edition first published 2006 by Book Blocks
an imprint of CRW Publishing Limited
69 Gloucester Crescent, London NW1 7EG

ISBN 1 904 919 73 1

1 3 5 7 9 10 8 6 4 2

Some of the data in this book has been extracted from
The Timechart History of Ireland

Written by Gill Davies
Typeset in Great Britain by Playne Books Limited
Printed and bound in China by Imago

Contents

Introducing Dublin and the Irish

Och, Dublin City, there is no doubtin',
Bates every city upon the say;
'Tis there you'll see O'Connell spoutin',
An' Lady Morgan makin' tay;
For 'tis the capital of the finest nation,
Wid charmin' pisintry on a fruitful sod,
Fightin' like divils for conciliation
An' hatin' each other for the love of God.
Charles James Lever

Ah, Ireland. . . That damnable, delightful country,
where everything that is right is the opposite
of what it ought to be
Benjamin Disraeli

The English language brings out the best in the Irish. They court it like a beautiful woman. They make it bray with donkey laughter. They hurl it at the sky like a paint pot full of rainbows, and then make it chant a dirge for man's fate and man's follies that is as mournful as misty spring rain crying over the fallow earth.

T E Kalem

after seeing Brendan Behan's play *Borstal Boy*

Author James Joyce gave the word 'Quark' to the English language.

Almost one third of the Republic of Ireland's population live in Dublin.

Palm trees can grow in Dublin. Even though the city lies at the same latitude as central Canada, the Gulf Stream warms its coastal water, so the weather is milder than one might suppose.

One late member of the Parliament claimed that there had been no sex in Ireland before television!

The world's first submarine, the *Fenian Ram,* was invented by John Philip Holland (1841–1914) who was born in County Clare.

In 1994, Eamonn Coghlan became the first person in the world over 40 years of age to succeed in running a mile in under 4 minutes.

The 'discovery' of America is attributed to Saint Brendan, a 6th-century Irish monk.

Dublin fish-and-chip shop owner, Ivan Beshoff, did not die until 1987, aged 104.

Author of *Gulliver's Travels*, Jonathan Swift (1667–1745), was dean of St Patrick's Cathedral.

The Gaelic name for Dublin (Baile Atha Cliath) means 'Town of the Ford of the Hurdles'.

The world's first tank, used at the Battle of the Somme in 1916, was co-designed by Dubliner, Walter Gordon Wilson (1874–1957).

Ernest Walton, educated at Trinity College, Dublin, and winner of the Nobel Prize for Physics, designed the world's first nuclear particle generator, and is credited with first splitting the atom in 1931.

Outstanding soldiers born in Ireland have included Lord Kitchener, Lawrence of Arabia and Field Marshal Montgomery.

Robert Boyle, the scientist who discovered the relationship between the pressure, volume and temperature of a gas (Boyle's Law) has his own niche as part of the impressive Boyle Family Monument in St Patrick's Cathedral.

The Joshua Tree by the Irish group, U2, became the fastest-selling album in British pop music history in 1987.

The inaugural performance of Handel's *Messiah* took place in Dublin in 1742.

In its early days, Dublin had a large slave market. Thralls were captured and sold, not only by the Norse but also by warring Irish chiefs.

The Dublin Millennium fifty-pence coin was minted in 1988 even though it was realised that by then Dublin had existed for well over 1,000 years.

Dublin is second only to Paris as the city to have produced most winners of the Nobel Prize for Literature (including W.B. Yeats, George Bernard Shaw, Samuel Beckett and Seamus Heaney).

Dublin is home to many theatres and cinemas. In fact, Ireland has the highest rate of cinema attendance in the whole of Europe.

Irish actor, Peter O'Toole (who appeared in a Dublin production of *Waiting for Godot* in 1971), is the actor who has received the most Academy Award nominations (7 for best actor) without ever actually winning one of these prestigious awards.

English rule began in the 1100s.
Since then the city of Dublin has served as the capital of Ireland under the:
Lordship of Ireland (1171–1541)
Kingdom of Ireland (1541–1801)
United Kingdom of Great Britain and Ireland (1801–1922)
Irish Republic (1919–1922).

From 1921, following the partition of Ireland, Dublin has served as the capital of Southern Ireland (1921–1922) and the Irish Free State (1922–1937).

Saint Patrick

The world's first ladies' tennis championship was played in Dublin in 1879.

Caibre, the MGM lion who roars and snarls at the beginning of their movies, was raised in Dublin Zoo in Phoenix Park.

The full name of Oscar Wilde (born 21 Westland Row, Dublin) was Oscar Fingal O'Flahertie Wills Wilde.

Ireland's patron saint, Saint Patrick, was probably Welsh – one missionary Maewyn Succat, who may have founded a church on the site of St Patrick's Cathedral.

It was Saint Patrick who used the shamrock to represent the Holy Trinity and this has been Ireland's national emblem ever since.

When Cromwell invaded Dublin in 1649, he used St Patrick's cathedral as a stable.

Flesh fishing! Bodysnatchers in early 18th-century Dublin used to steal fresh corpses by hooking them up under their chins and dragging them up out of the ground again to sell to medical students.

Fishamble Street in the Temple Bar area follows the path of a Viking route and is the oldest street in Dublin.

Guinness facts and figures

The Guinness Brewery is probably the city's most famous business, founded in 1759 in St James's Street. Today Arthur Guinness Son & Co still produces its dark beer at the same St James's Gate Brewery.

In 1759, Arthur Guinness signed an incredibly long 9,000-year lease for the brewery at just £45 per annum – now a ludicrously low rate for a site in the middle of one of the most sought-after and expensive areas of the city.

2.5 million pints of the famous dark stout are brewed daily (more than half the total amount drunk in Ireland).

Guinness is one of Ireland's largest employers and exporters.

Guinness is the world's largest single-beer exporter, exporting some 300 million pints each year.

The word 'stout' became the name for the Guinness beer in the 1820s.

Recent advertising campaigns state that, 'It takes 119.5 seconds to pour the perfect pint of Guinness with a head just proud of the rim of the glass'.

The St James Gate Guinness brewery now covers 64 acres.

Do all the bubbles travel downwards in a pint of Guinness?

No: but, in any beer, the upward flow of those bubbles which touch the walls of a glass slows down – while the bubbles in the centre of the glass are free to rise to the surface in a column. This creates a vortex, so the bubbles near the edge of the glass are sucked downwards.

As the bubbles in Guinness rise and fall with the vortex effect this is more obvious than in other beers because it has light-coloured bubbles in a dark-coloured liquid.

Is it true that that Guinness is brewed with water from the River Liffey, which flows through Dublin, close to St James's Gate?
No: it actually comes from the Wicklow Mountains, at Lady's Well.

Bartenders who want to impress their customers sometimes try to draw
the shamrock or harp logo of the Guinness company on the frothy head of the stout.

In the 1980s, after some disputes, the family presence on the board declined and today no Guinness sits on the board of the holding company, Diageo PLC.

Today's Guinness Original or Extra Stout is the draft that is closest to Arthur Guinness's original porter.

Guinness adopted the harp as a logo in 1862 but this faces left (its faces right in the coat of arms).

The grandson of the original Arthur Guinness, Sir Benjamin Guinness, became a Lord Mayor of Dublin and was made a baronet in 1867.

Guinness fans can visit the Guinness Storehouse in Dublin, which has been described as 'Disneyland for stout lovers'.

Guinness's famous advertising was devised by Benson's in the 1930s and 1940s.

John Gilroy was responsible for creating a series of posters which included such phrases as, 'Guinness is Good For You'.

The renowned Guinness posters often featured animals such as a kangaroo, lion, ostrich, seal and – most famously – a toucan.

By September 2005, the St James Gate brewery had been expanded allow all the Guinness in Ireland and the UK to be produced at the site.

The 2005 expansion at the brewery was expected to bring a 50% increase in beer production with an output of up to 3 million pints a day.

A pint of Guinness is recommended as a 'cure' for overindulging the night before.

The Guinness company also produced *The Guinness Book of Records,* which originated in 1955 when an argument in a pub was unable to be settled by any of the reference books then available.

Dublin History

Prehistory

The Antrim coast of Ireland was at one time linked to Scotland by a landbridge.

The landbrige was eroded before adders moved north in Britain, so there are no snakes in the Dublin area – or anywhere else in Ireland – although sometimes Saint Patrick is claimed to have sent them packing!

At Newgrange, north of Dublin, ancient burial mounds date to 3100 BCE, predating Egyptian pyramids.

8,000 BCE

The area of Dublin ciy and its surroundings was now inhabited.

100s

Ireland is the most westerly point in Europe ever reached by settlers or traders. The earliest real settlement in Dublin appeared in or before the early 100s.

The first settlement on the River Liffey was called Eblana, later referred to as Eblana Civitas.

c. 140

The first *recorded* reference to a settlement in the Dublin area was in the writings of Claudius Ptolemaeus (usually called Ptolemy), the Greek-born Egyptian geographer, astronomer and cartographer. However, the settlement had existed well before Ptolemy actually wrote about it.

432–461

Saint Patrick (probably a Welsh missionary, Maewan Succat) converted Ireland to Christianity.

Celt in war dress

800

The wonderful illuminated *Book of Kells* was made.

800s

The Danes first arrived to raid the Dublin area.

The Viking, Ivar the Boneless and Olaf, King of Dublin, captured Dumbarton in Scotland.

841

The Norse Vikings built their first settlement in Dublin, from whence they raided surrounding areas.

Viking warrior

Early 900s

Norman Viking settlement was developed and called An Dubh Linn (meaning Black Pool) or Dyflin by the Vikings. This was located in the area now known as Wood Quay (in the present city centre).

The Celtic settlement, Áth Cliath (meaning 'hurdle ford'), was set a little further upriver from An Dubh Linn.

902

Vikings in Dublin were defeated and temporarily driven out.

917

Vikings return to Dublin, led by Sitric Gale.

919

Niall Húndub the Blackkneed, High King of Tara, tried to expel the Dublin Vikings.
Niall Húndub was killed in the attempt to repel the Viking attack on Dublin.

921

Godfrid became King of Dublin. His son Olaf will succeed to this title.

937

King Olaf was defeated by the Anglo Saxons and Athelstan at Brunanburh.

944

Dublin was sacked by Uí Néill and the Men of Leinster. Olaf Cuáran became King of Dublin.

980

The new high king captured Dublin after a three-day seige and freed many slaves. The city was looted.

989

Sitric Silkenbeard began his reign as King of Dublin and minted the first Irish coins.

1013

The Dublin Ostmen revolted against Brian Boru, now King of Ireland.

1014

Viking power is undermined (but they still hold on for a while) with their defeat by the Irish High King, Brian Boru, at the battle of Clontarf on Good Friday.

Brian Boru at the battle of Clontarf

1028

Sitric, King of Dublin, went on a pilgrimage to Rome and would found Christchurch Cathedral on his return.

1029

Olaf, son of Sitric and now King of Dublin, was kidnapped. His ransom was set at 1,200 cows, 120 horses and 60 ounces of gold.

1030

Sitric, Christian king of Dublin's norsemen, founded Christchurch Cathedral at the Viking settlement of Wood Quay, by the River Liffey quayside.

1052

Dublin's first native Irish king was Diarmait Mac Maelnamó.

1052,1075, and 1124

The Irish managed to seize Dublin back again from the Danes.

1166

Henry II of England offered to help the King of Leinster (whose territory included Dublin) resist a neighbouring king's attacks.

The king of Leinster promised overlordship of Leinster – plus his eldest daughter – to whomsoever led an invasion against his enemies.

1170

The Danes were expelled by the Anglo-Normans, led by the Earl of Pembroke, Richard de Clare (Strongbow) under Henry II, King of England.

1171

Henry II proclaimed Dublin to be under his control.

From 1171 onwards Dublin was peopled extensively with settlers from England and Wales. The rural area around the city, as far north as Drogheda, now saw extensive English settlement.

1172

Henry II of England came to Dublin and held his court here.

King Henry II granted the government of Dublin to

Hugh de Lacy and and 'to his subjects of Bristol his city of Dublin to inhabit'.

1172–73

Strongbow (Richard de Clare, Second Earl of Pembroke) and invader of Ireland, began the construction of Christchurch Cathedral in Dublin (founded 1028). Strongbow's tomb now rests here.

900s–1200s

Notwithstanding several battles and defeats from 936 onwards, the Vikings (or Ostmen) would rule Dublin for almost three centuries.

1190

The cathedral of St Patrick was founded by John Comyn, archbishop of Dublin.

1200s

Dublin was now Ireland's centre of English power.

The Normans conquered the southern half of Ireland (Munster and Leinster).

Many of the Anglo-Norman conquerors were absorbed into the Irish culture, adopting the Irish language and customs.

1207

King John grants Dublin a fresh charter.

1209

300 Dubliners – men, women and children – were killed on Easter Sunday by the O'Byrnes and O'Tooles in Cullenswood.

1216

Henry III granted Magna Carta to the Irish and the fee farm of Dublin was granted to the citizens at 200 marks per annum.

1227

Henry III confirmed the charter and fixed the city boundaries of Dublin.

Late 1200s

A population of 5,000 lived in congested quarters within the city walls, where fire and disease were constant threats. Drinking water was filthy.

1295

Severe food shortages. Even the gallows were sometimes robbed as a source of meat.

1311

Dublin had permission from the Pope to establish a university.

1315

Edward and Robert Bruce of Scotland invaded Ireland with 6,000 men but failed to take Dublin.

Dublin's citizens burned the suburbs – the entire western part of the city – to prevent their city falling into enemy hands. Some demolished their homes in order to use the debris to shore up the city walls.

1315–1317

Death, famine and ruin followed the seige. There are tales of starving people going mad and digging up graves to eat the corpses and women resorting to eating their own babies. Much of this is the stuff of legend, but the starvation was a real horror.

1348

The population of Dublin was now nearly 5,000.

1348

The Black Death ravaged Ireland. Medieval Dublin

was hit particularly badly in 1348 – and victims were buried in mass graves in an area still known as 'Blackpitts'.

1383

Once again, bubonic plague raged in Ireland.

1394

English King Richard II entered Dublin and held a Parliament there.

1400

King Richard II of England visited Dublin again.

1405

First historic reference to Irish whiskey when an Irish lord died from an excess of it!

1430

Parliament grants Dublin money towards the building of Dublin Castle.

King Richard II's fleet:
he visited Dublin in 1394 and 1400

1439

Dublin again suffered as plague invaded the city.

1446

Dublin's city charter allowed 'chirurgery': barber surgeons could practise.

A small area around Dublin, known as the Pale, had stayed under direct English control. People outside this area were still considered savage, giving rise to the expression, 'Beyond the Pale'.

1480

Plague struck the city yet again.

1487

The English pretender to the Crown, Lambert Simnel, was crowned at Christchurch as Edward VI.

1487

English pretender, Lambert Simnel, was defeated at the Battle of Stoke; the harmless dupe of others, who sought power through him, was let off to become a scullion in the royal kitchens and a falconer.

1500

By now Dublin had about 9,000 residents. Town life was busy and chaotic.

1531

Reformation in England. Henry VIII seizes the opportunity to take church land in Ireland and give it to his supporters.

1534

Lord Thomas Fitzgerald led a rebellion against the English and attacked Dublin.

Henry VIII, King of England and Ireland

1536

Henry VIII was made supreme spiritual Head of the Church in Ireland and would become king of Ireland in 1541.

Mid 1500s

Monastery lands were seized under the Reformation but the new religious ideas were not greatly preached outside Dublin's city boundaries.

1536 and 1539

Acts of Parliament dissolved Dublin's monasteries.

1541

Dublin's Parliament had many Gaelic chiefs, now made earls by Henry VIII as he assumed his role as Head of the Church and King of Ireland.

1558

Queen Elizabeth's reign began. She set out to 'civilize Ireland and its barbarous people'.

Many icons and relics were taken from the city's churches. A wooden staff supposedly given to Dublin by Saint Patrick (the Bacall Iosa) was ritually burned.

Queen Elizabeth I

1560

Ireland was proclaimed an Anglican country by the English. Protestants seized the Catholic churches and Catholics worshipped in cellars.

1576

One third of the population died in the Black Death.

The Guild of Barbers was united with the Dublin surgeons by royal charter.

Late 1500s

Trinity College was founded on the site of a priory in 1591–92.

Dublin grew rapidly as great numbers of Protestant refugees from Europe arrived. By 1600 the population was some 10,000.

1600s

Throughout this century, the English Tudor kings and then their successors, Cromwell and the Stuarts, brought their armies over to Ireland and strengthened the English control of the nation.

Hoggen Green (from the Scandinavian word for a mound and the nearby nunnery) was renamed College Green.

By contrast to the growth in wealth, Dublin's poor suffered with the supression of the Catholic Church as its charitable organisations were no longer able to offer support and help or to clean the city and make living conditions better.

Dublin's size and wealth expanded until it was called the second city of the British Empire.

1603

All city officers, including those in Dublin, had to take the Oath of Supremacy and Uniformity.

1611

The first licence for a public house was granted.

1642–46

The English Civil War brought splits and opportunities for rebellion in Ireland. However, despite conspiracies to seize Dublin Castle, it remained a Royalist stronghold.

English troops at Dublin Castle

1646

There were risings among the Irish outside Dublin and they (unsuccessfully) besieged the city in 1646.

1649

As Roman Catholic worship was forbidden under Cromwell's rule, many priests fled elsewhere or went into hiding. Many of those caught were killed.

After the English Civil War, Oliver Cromwell, with 12,000 men, landed in Dublin on 15 August as commander in chief under the parliament.

1649

Cromwell and his Model Army took over the small, walled medieval town of Dublin and then, from this vantage point, fiercely suppressed the Irish. His army went on to murder 3,000 people in one night in Drogheda and 2,000 one day in Wexford.

The last major plague outbreak in Dublin. It had recurred regularly in the city for some 300 years.

Mid 1600s

Under Cromwell's fierce regime, 15million acres of land were seized from Catholic landowners.

Dublin was pronounced by the English to be overwhelmingly Protestant.

1650–1700

Some 10,000 Huguenots arrived, fleeing persecution in Europe. They developed poplin and silk-weaving industries and encouraged the wine trade.

1665

The Monarchy had been restored in England. The Mayor of Dublin became a Lord Mayor now.

Following the Restoration, the Duke of Ormond was appointed Lord Deputy of Ireland.

1689

James II landed in Ireland after being expelled from England and held a parliament in Dublin.

1690

James II returned for just a few hours after his defeat at the Battle of the Boyne but the very next day William III proceeded in state to St Patrick's cathedral to give thanks for his victory.

1700s

Dublin's prosperity attracted the Protestant Ascendancy. Many of these members of the Anglo-Irish aristocracy denied basic civil rights to the local Roman Catholics.

Roman Catholics could neither vote nor stand for Parliament, hold an office of state, buy land, practise law or join the armed forces.

Dublin's narrow medieval streets were replaced by wide neo-classical roads with many fine parks and squares. Temple Bar developed.

Architect James Gandon designed Custom House, the Kings Inns and Four Courts and oversaw the development of Gardiner Street.

1702

Marsh's Library was built.

Trinity College Library was begun.

1710

Trinity College medical school was founded with a theatre of anatomy and a fine herb garden.

1713

Jonathan Swift (author of *Gulliver's Travels* published in *1726)* became Dean of St Patrick's.

1731

The new Parliament House was opened.

1739–41

Major Irish famine in which 400,000 died.

Jonathan Swift

1741–42

George Frederick Handel lived in Dublin's Abbey Street.

1752

Work commenced on Trinity College's new façade, considered the greatest piece of collegiate architecture in Europe at that time.

1757

Dean Swift helped to found St Patrick's Hospital for Imbeciles.

1759

Arthur Guinness launched his famous brewery at St James's Gate.

1770s

A golden age for Dublin culture with great achievements in publishing, music and theatre. Sheridan, Congreve and Goldsmith all lived and worked in Dublin, as did philosopher Edmund Burke and author Dean Swift.

The play, *The Rivals*, was staged at Covent Garden, London. Its author Richard Brinsley Sheridan was Dublin born.

1776

American Civil War: Irish troops sent to America.

Late 1700s

By now the Catholics owned a mere 5% of land in Ireland and there was much dissent in Dublin.

Animosity between Protestants and Catholics began to erupt into sectarian violence as the Liberty Boys (Protestant tailors' apprentices) fought the Ormond Boys (Catholic butchers' assistants).

1780s

As a result of the many disturbances and conspiracies in Dublin, Volunteers pressed for parliamentary reform.

1782

Henry Grattan, politician, won Ireland's legislative independence from England's Privy Council. Some (but not all) of the anti-Catholic legislation was repealed.

Ireland was now a nation.

Dublin Volunteers:

Great strife in the city

1793

For the first time, Roman Catholics were allowed to attend Trinity College.

1797

Orange Lodge was formed in Dublin.

1798

Irish Catholics rebelled, seeking reforms, many inspired by American and French revolutionary ideals. Helped by French troops, the United Irishmen led the rebellion.

Rebels tried to seize the city of Dublin but were ferociously suppressed. Some 30,000 people died.

Dublin's Wolfe Tone who had orchestrated the rebellion, was captured but he committed suicide, slitting his throat with a penknife before he could be executed.

Lord Edward Fitzgerald, senior officer in Ireland, was captured and killed 4 days before the planned date of the rebellion and Robert Emmet fled to France where he would gather support for further action.

The arrest of Lord Fitzgerald

1800

The Act of Union between England and Ireland abolished the Irish Parliament.

As the new political order under the Act of Union swung into action, it drastically reduced the status of Dublin.

Daniel O'Connell made his first public speech to protest against the Act of Union – at Dublin's Royal Exchange.

1800s

A long decline set in that would not be be reversed until Southern Ireland gained its full independence in 1922.

1803

Robert Emmet led an insurrection; this was quelled in just one afternoon. Emmet was tried and hanged.

1834

The railway from Dublin to Kingstown was the world's first suburban rail line.

1839

During the Night of the Big Wind, 5,000 houses were damaged or destroyed in the city. 1,000s of trees were blown down.

The General Post Office, Dublin, was opened to the public.

1842

The *Nation* newspaper was founded in Dublin.

Daniel O'Connell

1843

Daniel O'Connell, first Catholic Lord Mayor of Dublin, led demands for repeal of the Act of Union.

1845, 1846 and Black 47

The vital potato crops failed several times over. A great famine began that would continue into 1847 with repercussions far beyond that date.

1845–47

Many starved. While Irish landlords still shipped grain, cattle, pork, sheep, oats and flour to

England, famine victims died, not only through starvation but through disease too.

1845–51

Dropsy, dysentery, typhus, scurvy and cholera – all diseases accelerated by weakness and starvation – devastated the people of Ireland.

Many fled Ireland and the ravages of the famine, emigrating to England or America. Dublin's population drops from 8 million in 1841 to 6.5 million in 1851.

The potato famine led to mass emigration

1848

Great agitation and many disturbances followed in the wake of the famine but there was little bloodshed.

The green, white and orange tricolour was presented formally to the Irish people as their flag by Thomas Francis Magher, the Young Irelander.

1849

Queen Victoria visited Dublin.

British Prime Minister, Willam Gladstone, tried to help the Irish and to introduce Home Rule. He said, 'My mission is to pacify Ireland.'

1851

Dublin's population was now just under 250,000 but there were poor housing conditions and bad sanitation. Mortality rose.

1860s

As the Irish identity surged, the Fenian movement grew and spread – in Dublin City, in Ireland overall and among the Irish living in America and Canada.

1867

Fenian rising took place in Dublin (and other

cities) but this failed, in part due to heavy snowstorms.

When the Fenian conspiracy was discovered, the Habeas Corpus act was suspended and there were some 960 arrests in Dublin within a few hours.

Dublin castle was fortified and great fear reigned in the city for several weeks.

1882

Thomas Burke and Lord Frederick Cavendish were brutally murdered in Phoenix Park, Dublin, by the 'Invincibles' with surgical knives.

Charles Stuart Parnell

1846–1891

Charles Stuart Parnell, champion of nationalism and Home Rule leader, transformed Irish and British politics but his association with Kitty O'Shea (and ultimately her divorce in 1890) led to his downfall.

1907

The Abbey Theatre opened with plays by W. B. Yeats and Lady Gregory.

Performances of John M. Synge's T*he Playboy of the Western World* led to riots in the Abbey Theatre.

1909

The first cinema in Dublin opens, the *Volta*. James Joyce was its manager.

1914

World War I began in Europe. 200,000 Irish men volunteered. Thousands would die.

1916

Easter Rising 24–29 April

Rebel leaders signed a Proclamation of Independence. Volunteers occupied the Post Office and other central Dublin buildings.

Patrick Pearse read out the Proclamation of Independence on the steps of the General Post Office.

The Four Courts, St Stephens Green, Liberty Hall, Jacob's Biscuit Factory and Bolands Flour Mill were seized and occupied by the rebels.

Surrounded by British troops and bombarded by a gunboat, Dublin burned and suffered heavy gunfire. The rebels were forced to surrender.

THE PROCLAMATION OF

POBLACHT NA H EIREANN.

THE PROVISIONAL GOVERNMENT OF THE

IRISH REPUBLIC

TO THE PEOPLE OF IRELAND.

IRISHMEN AND IRISHWOMEN: In the name of God and the dead generations from which she receives her old tradition of nationhood, Ireland, through us, summons her children to her flag and strikes for her freedom.

Having organised and trained her manhood through her secret revolutionary organisation, the Irish Republican Brotherhood, and through her open military organisations, the Irish Volunteers and the Irish Citizen Army, having patiently perfected her discipline, having resolutely waited for the right moment to reveal itself, she now seizes that moment, and, supported by her exiled children in America and by gallant allies in Europe, but relying in the first on her own strength, she strikes in full confidence of victory.

We declare the right of the people of Ireland to the ownership of Ireland, and to the unfettered control of the Irish destinies, to be sovereign and indefeasible. The long usurpation of that right by a foreign people and government has not extinguished the right, nor can it ever be extinguished except by the destruction of the Irish people. In every generation the Irish people have asserted their right to national freedom and sovereignty : six times during the past three hundred years they have asserted it in arms. Standing on that fundamental right and again asserting it in arms in the face of the world, we hereby proclaim the Irish Republic as a Sovereign Independent State, and we pledge our lives and the lives of our comrades-in-arms to the cause of its freedom, of its welfare, and of its exhaltation among the nations.

The Irish Republic is entitled to, and hereby claims, the allegiance of every Irishman and Irishwoman. The Republic guarantees religious and civil liberty, equal rights and equal opportunities to all its citizens, and declares its resolve to pursue the happiness and prosperity of the whole nation and of all its parts, cherishing all the children of the nation equally, and oblivious of the differences carefully fostered by an alien government, which has divided a minority from the majority in the past.

Until our arms have brought the opportune moment for the establishment of a permanent National Government, representative of the whole people of Ireland and elected by the suffrages of all her men and women, the provisional Government, hereby constituted, will administer the civil and military affairs of the Republic in trust for the people.

We place the cause of the Irish Republic under the protection of the Most High God, Whose blessing we invoke upon our arms, and we pray that no one who serves that cause will dishonour it by cowardice, inhumanity, or rapine. In this supreme hour, the Irish nation must, by its valour and discipline and by the readiness of its children to sacrifice themselves for the common good, prove itself worthy of the august destiny to which it is called.

Signed on Behalf of the Provisional Government.

THOMAS J. CLARKE

SEAN Mac DIARMADA. THOMAS MacDONAGH.

P. H. PEARSE. EAMONN CEANNT.

JAMES CONNOLLY. JOSEPH PLUNKETT

After his arrest, Sir Roger Casement commented: *I came here for one thing only, to try to help national Ireland—and if there is no such thing in existence then the sooner I pay for my illusions the better.*

3–12 May

Sixteen of the Easter Rising rebels were shot.

77 death sentences were issued.

Post Easter Rising

Sir Roger Casement would be hanged in August.

Sir Roger Casement stated:

It is a strange, strange fate, and now, as I stand face to face with death, I feel just as if they were going to kill a boy. For I feel like a boy—and my hands are so free from blood and my heart always so compassionate and pitiful that I cannot comprehend that anyone wants to hang me.

July to November 1916

Many Irish soldiers were slaughtered in Europe in the Battle of the Somme.

1918

De Valera's new party Sinn Fein, won 75% of Irish seats in the British general election.

1919

The first ever Irish parliament (Dáil Eireann) met in the Mansion House in Dublin on 21 January.

1919-1921

A three-year period of struggle and fighting, during which both the IRA and the British soldiers (the Black and Tans) committed dire atrocities.

1920

On 21 November, 14 undercover British operatives were killed in their beds on the orders of Michael Collins.

Two IRA and one Sinn Fein supporter were executed at Dublin Castle.

On the same day that IRA and Sinn Fein supporters were executed, 12 people died when British troops fired on football spectators in Dublin's Croke Park.

1921

A truce was declared on 9 July when a delegation, led by Michael Collins, met the British government.

Six Ulster counties would not join the Irish Free State so Ireland split – geographically, politically and on religious grounds.

6 December

Anglo-Irish treaty conferred dominion status on 26 of Ireland's 32 counties and created the foundation for the Irish Free State.

April 1922

A War of Independence: Dublin (especially the Four Courts and GPO areas) was the scene of some of the most severe fighting during the Irish Civil War which ultimately led to the establishment of the Irish Free State.

August 1922

With the deaths of their leaders, the Provisional Government under Michael Collins and the de facto Irish Republic under the President of Dáil Éireann, (Arthur Griffith) in effect, merged.

August 22nd, 1922

Michael Collins was shot dead in his car. His body lay in state in Dublin for three days. Thousands paid their respects and lined the streets for his funeral procession.

December 1922

Irish Free State came into being, replacing the two co-existing but nominally rival states. The structures were laid out in the Treaty and Constitution. It created a constitutional monarchy, with a three-tier parliament, made up of the King and two houses, Dáil Éireann and Seanad Éireann (the Irish Senate).

1923

After the civil war, as Ireland gained its independence, Dublin now became the political, economic, and cultural centre of Ireland.

1923–1924-1926

Sean O'Casey's *The Shadow of a Gunman* and *Juno and the Paycock* were produced at the Abbey Theatre. The opening of the *Plough and the Stars* was marked by rioting.

1923

The Government of Ireland, Dáil Éireann, assembled in Leinster House, Dublin.

De Valera had split off from the republicans to form Fianna Fáil (Warriors of Ireland) and won as many seats as the government.

1926

Ireland's first radio station broadcast from an office in Little Denmark Street

1930s onwards

Troubles in Northern Ireland impacted on Dublin plus ballot rigging and voter intimidation.

1932–1948

Eamon de Valera, leader of the Civil War's anti-treaty forces, was elected and served for 16 years as Taoiseach. He promoted Ireland's independence.

1930s

Jews, fleeing Nazi persecution in Europe, arrived to swell Dublin's small Jewish community.

Eamon de Valera

1934

The Irish Free State sent a team to the British Empire Games in London.

1937

Eamon de Valera, who had been promoting Ireland's independence through a trade war with Britain, now set up the new constitution.

The free state was now formally called Eire.

1939

One faction of the IRA stole a large amount of the Irish Army's reserve ammunition in a raid on the Magazine Fort in Dublin's Phoenix Park.

1939

After the IRA raid on Dublin's Magazine Fort, De Valera interned and executed some IRA members.

1939–45

World War II: Dublin escaped heavy bombing and air raids during World War II due to Ireland's neutrality. There were, however, food shortages and rationing.

May 1941

German bombs hit the north wall of the north inner city. Overall, the war took 30 lives and caused about 80 casualties in Ireland.

1948

Fianna Fáil ousted.

1949

On Easter Monday, Ireland (minus the 6 counties) left the British Commonwealth.

Now at last Ireland could be declared a Republic.

1950s

Many 18th-century houses were demolished, notably in Fitzwilliam Street and St Stephen's Green, to create space for new building projects – mainly office blocks and government departments.

Great economic migration, especially to the UK, as 40,000 people a year left Ireland.

1950s–60s

Strict censorhip laws drove away many authors and culture was cramped as works were banned by such Irish writers as Brendan Behan, Edna O'Brien, George Bernard Shaw and Samuel Beckett.

As well as Irish writers, many international authors' works were banned under the censorship rulings. These included Noel Coward, Dylan Thomas and Ernest Hemingway.

The works of many authors, including George Bernard Shaw, were banned.

1963

President John F Kennedy, of Irish descent, visited Ireland in the summer before his assassination in Dallas. He spoke in Dublin on 28 June and joined with Irish President Eamon de Valera to form the American Irish Foundation.

1966

On the 50th anniversary of the Easter Rising, Nelson's Pillar, Dublin, was destroyed by an IRA explosion – blown up by a small bomb shortly before the commemorations were due to begin.

1972

After the Bloody Sunday killings on 30 January in Derry, 30,000 protestors laid seige to Dublin's British Embassy for 3 days and then set it alight and burned it down.

1973

Ireland joined the European Economic Community.

1974

Explosions and multiple killings in May in Dublin.

1976

The British ambassador was killed in Dublin.

1979

The first ever papal visit to Ireland as Pope John Paul II arrived in September.

In the face of national opposition, Wood Quay – where the oldest remains of Viking Dublin were located – was demolished by the Dublin Corporation to be replaced with civic offices and the HQ of Dublin's local government.

1980s

The regeneration of Dublin saw the preservation of its architectural heritage and development of Temple Bar, with its original medieval street plan. Here artists gathered and created a lively cultural quarter.

Late 1980s

Parts of Grafton and Henry Streets pedestrianised.

1990s

Dublin saw a cultural surge. Many artists and musicians flocked to the city. They were able to make the most of a taxation system especially favourable to artists.

1990s

Pop stars – including most famously U2 – paid vast sums for properties on the south coast of the city and for exclusive hotel accommodation.

1990

Dublin Castle received huge EU funds for refurbishment in preparation for its hosting the European Parliament.

1992

Mary Robinson (elected 1990) was the first Irish President to visit Belfast.

1998

In April, a 68-page agreement on social, political and economic future of Ireland was signed.

Tony Blair became the first British PM to address the Dáil.

US President Clinton visited Dublin.

Late 1990s

Dublin had a building boom – plus the development of a financial district along the North Quays. Building values and rents rocketed.

1999

The Republic joined the European currency.

1990s

Many Dubliners left the city to settle in cheaper accommodation in counties Meath, Louth, Kildare and Wicklow, but still commuted daily into Dublin.

1990s–2003

Economic boom attracted immigrants from all over the world. Many Irish emigrants returned. Chinese, Nigerians, Russians, Romanians and others from Africa and eastern Europe arrived.

2003

Nelson's Pillar, the former landmark destroyed in 1966, was replaced by the Dublin Spire erected on the same spot.

The Dail allowed US planes to use Shannon airport. 100,000 protested against the Iraq war in Dublin.

Dublin was identified as the sixth best city in Europe and the 30th best in the world by Mercer Human Resources.

2004

Ireland took on the rotating presidency of the European Union.

2005

In October, Intelligence reports indicated that the IRA had fulfilled their promise to decommision weapons and end violence, the NI secretary reported.

Gerry Adams quote . . .

Making peace, I have found, is much harder than making war.

Dublin History

A fun way to learn all about Dublin's history and Irish tales is by taking a tour on a red city sightseeing bus. The guided tour, with many stops located at the more popular attractions, lasts about 1 hour 15 minutes. Visitors can hop on and off as often as they wish.

Buildings

The Abbey Theatre

The Abbey Theatre opened in 1904, dedicated to the revival of Irish drama with its co-founders and first directors W. B. Yeats and Lady Gregory.

Here plays by Yeats, J. M. Synge, Sean O'Casey, Brian Friel and Frank McGuiness have had their premieres, some causing controversy and even riots.

Lady Isabella Augusta Gregory 1852-1932 was a friend and collaborator of W. B. Yeats, with whom she formed the Irish Literary Theatre before renting the historic Abbey Theatre. A gifted writer and playwright, she was also a gatherer of old Irish folklore, songs and poems.

Archbishop Narcissus Marsh's Library

This is Ireland's first public library and was built in 1701.

The Archbishop's Library was given to the city by the archbishop who oversaw the first translation of the Old Testament into Irish.

The Library houses 25,000 old leather-bound volumes, the earliest from 1400.

The Bank of Ireland

These prestigious offices of the national bank are housed in the former Parliament House, set on College Green. Parliament House was sold to the Bank of Ireland for £40,000 in 1803.

The magnificent former House of Lords

This has a Waterford glass chandelier with 1,223 pieces of crystal, plus wonderful tapestries – and ushers in elegant costumes.

Casino Marino

Just off the Malahide Road, 3 miles north of the centre of Dublin. The Casino (meaning small house) was designed by Sir William Chambers and commissioned as a pleasure house by Lord Charlemont, the 1st Earl of that name.

The Casino

This is an extravagent 18th-century neo-classical building with urns that conceal chimneys, carved drapery, and sixteen finely decorated rooms.

Central Bank

Near Trinity College, this is a conrtroversial modern building, designed by Sam Stephenson, with elaborate architecture.

Christchurch Cathedral

The first timber cathedral was founded by Sitric Silkenbeard in about 1038 when Dublin was a Viking settlement in Ireland.

Christchurch was extensively rebuilt by the Anglo-Norman invaders of the late 1100s. Strongbow raised a stone building in 1172.

Christchurch Cathedral

Unfortunately Strongbow (Richard de Clare) built the building on a peat bog and so one wall tumbled down in 1562.

Christchurch was restored again in the 1870s.

Strongbow (Richard de Clare) is said to be buried in Christchurch but probably it is just his bowels that are interred here.

St Lawrence O'Toole's heart hangs on the wall in an iron casket. He was an archbishop of Dublin—1132–1180 – but died in Normandy.

Christchurch has a fine crypt which in medieval times doubled as a tavern!

Viking and Norman artefacts from Wood Quay are on display in Christchurch, along with reconstructions of a merchant's house and a gruesome Black Death scene.

The bells of Christchurch Cathedral are claimed to be 'the largest full-circle ringing peal in the world'.

Whiskey-maker Henry Roe is to be thanked for his restoration of the cathedral in 1871, especially as this left him bankrupt.

City Hall, Dame Street

This was formerly the Royal Exchange, built between 1769 and 1779 – a square building in Corinthian style, with fine Portland stone.

Since 1852, City Hall has been the centre of the municipal government.

Clery's Hotel

Formerly the Imperial Hotel, here Jim Larkin made his stirring trade unionist speech during 1913s general strike.

Clontarf Castle

Off Castle Avenue Clontarf
The castle stands where the Knights Templar (later of the Knights Hospitaller of St John of Jerusalem) held command in medieval times.

Custom House

Custom House Quay
This is a James Gandon masterpiece with its foundations set on a layer of pine planks in the muddy River Liffey banks.

Custom House is one of Dublin's finest Georgian

buildings. It was set on fire by Republicans in 1921 and burned for 5 days but was impeccably restored.

Dublin Castle

Palace Street, off Dame Street Set south of the river, this is one of the most ancient structures in the city and was begun in 1204.

By 1207, it served as the first Dublin court of King John. It was almost totally rebuilt in Georgian style in the 1700s.

The castle was the seat of English power in Ireland for over 700 years until 1922 when it came under the jurisdiction of the Irish Free State.

Today Ireland's presidents are inaugurated in Dublin Castle.

In the Chester Beatty Library are ancient manuscripts that date back to Biblical times plus copies of the Koran and Christian scrolls.

Outside the gates of Dublin Castle on Dame Street is the headquarters of 'The Sick and Indigent Roomkeepers Society', founded in 1790 and still attracting membership!

The Four Courts

Arran Quay

Standing near the north bank of the River Liffey on the west side of Dublin is the seat of Ireland's judiciary and an excellent example of Dublin's fine late 18th-century architecture.

The Four Courts has been home to the Irish law courts since 1796. The buildings were damaged heavily during the Civil War but have been well restored.

The Four Courts

The Gate Theatre

The Gate Theatre was founded in 1925. In their earliest days, theatrical productions in Dublin sometimes served political purposes and The Gate was no exception.

General Post Office (GPO)

O'Connell Street
This opened in 1818 on what was then Sackville Street and was designed by Francis Johnston.

The GPO became a symbol of the 1916 Easter Rising for it served as the rebel headquarters during the battle for independence.

Here Patrick Pearse stood on the steps to read the Declaration of a free Irish Republic.

Much of the façade of the General Post Office was destroyed in the ensuing battle and those parts of the building that survived show many bullet scars to this day.

Government Buildings

Merrion Street Upper
The offices of the Government Departments are open to the public at certain times.

The Green Building

This experimental building has a roof made of propellers and solar panels with balustrades made from old bicycle frames.

Kilmainham Gaol

This gaol held many a felon from its opening in 1798 until 1924 when the new Free State government ordered that it should be closed.

Here were incarcerated many nationalist rebels including United Irishmen from 1798, Parnell and

Davitt in 1883, plus Pádraig Pearce and James Connolly after the 1916 Easter Rising.

Pádraig Pearce and James Connolly were executed in the prison yard of Kilmainham Gaol.

After the Easter Rising, one of its leaders, Joseph Plunkett, was married (to Grace Gifford) in Kilmainham Gaol while British soldiers stood to attention. Two hours later, after being allowed only ten minutes with his new wife, he was executed.

The very last prisoner was Eamon de Valera, who was released in July 1924.

The 'museum' displays here evoke the atmosphere of the gaol that was not altered after its 1924 closure and bring to life the grim conditions; there is even a multimedia display on hanging.

Kings Inns

In 1795 this classically proportioned building was founded as a place of residence and study for barristers. It was designed by James Gandon.

The building was finally completed in 1817 after Francis Johnston had added its graceful cupola. The gardens are open to the public but the building is open only to members of the legal profession.

Leinster House

Kildare Street
This building was originally built as a town house for the Duke of Leinster in 1745.

The government gained Leinster House in 1922 for parliamentary use and then bought the entire building two years later for the Irish Parliament and the Senate. Here Parliament sits for 90 days a year.

The building is home to the National Museum and the National Library.

The building was the inspiration for the design of the White House in Washington.

Liberty Hall

This is Dublin's tallest building and the heart of trade unionism here since 1913 when Jim Larkin and the Irish Trade and General Workers Union acquired it.

Mansion House

Dawson Street
Built 1710, this has been the official residence of the mayor since 1715. The Dáil Éireann first met

here on 21 January 1919, before moving to Leinster House.

Today Mansion House with its delicate style but heavy Victorian wrought iron, hosts many civic functions and receptions.

Newman House

85–86 St Stephens Green
Dublin's second-oldest university (after Trinity) is University College. This has now moved to the suburbs but the Catholic University of Ireland had its first premises here.

It was in Newman House that the poet and Jesuit priest, Gerald Manley Hopkins (1884–89) had a chair and was professor of classics.

Pádraig Pearse, Eamon de Valera and James Joyce were graduates of Newman House.

The rather daring female nudes on the interior plasterwork was covered up when Newman House became part of the Catholic University.

Number Twenty Nine

29 Lower Fitzwilliam Street
This unique museum is a restored four-storey town

house in the heart of what was once Dublin's most fashionable Georgian area. It exhibits the lifestyle of a Dublin middle-class family during the period 1790 to 1820.

The house was rebuilt by the Electricity Board, who knocked it down in the first place, along with 25 other Georgian houses.

Parliament House

Parliament House was set on College Green in the building that is now The Bank of Ireland. In former times, this was the first purpose-built parliament house erected in Europe.

Completed in 1739, the fine Georgian-style Parliament House served as Ireland's Parliament until the Act Of Union in 1801.

Powerscourt Townhouse Centre

South William Street
Once the townhouse of a Georgian family, the building was restored in the 1960s into a fine shopping centre with jewellery and antique shops.

Royal Hospital Kilmainham

With its colonnades, central courtyard and fine stone arcarding, this was Ireland's very first

Classical building in 1680 – when it was built as a home for wounded army officers.

Royal College of Surgeons

St Stephens Green West
Built in 1806, this imposing building was commandeered by Irish Volunteers in the 1916 Easter Rising. Its columns still bear the pockmarks of bullets from the fighting.

Saint Anne's Church

This has a beautiful ornate Italianate façade. Behind the altar are wooden shelves designed to hold loaves of bread for poor parishioners in response to a 1720s bequest.

Author Bram Stoker was married in 1878 in Saint Anne's Church.

Saint Michan's Church

Church Street Lower
A place of worship since 1096, its vaults contain the mummified bodies of a crusader, a nun and a thief.

The death mask of the charismatic Irish patriot, Theobald Wolfe Tone (1763–1798) rests here.

Handel may have practised The Messiah *on the organ at St Michan's Church.*

Handel is reputed to have practised his *Messiah* on the organ here before the first performance in Dublin.

The philosopher Edmund Burke was christened here.

This was where the funeral of Home Rule leader Charles Stewart Parnell took place.

Saint Patrick's Cathedral

This is Dublin's second Protestant cathedral, built just after Christchurch in about 1190 and dating from Dublin's earliest days as a Viking settlement.

Saint Patrick's Cathedral

This is the largest church in Ireland and one of the most famous in the world.

The cathedral was extensively reconstructed by successive invaders through the 1100s and early 1200s and rebuilt again in the 1800s.

Legend has it that Saint Patrick baptized Christian converts within the grounds of Saint Patrick's.

Jonathan Swift, dean and author, is buried near the entrance, next to his mistress, Stella.

To make peace with each other, feuding earls, Kildare and Ormonde, shook hands through a hole cut in an old wooden chapter door at Saint Patrick's. The fact that they did so without incurring injury gave rise to the phrase 'chancing your arm'.

A St Patrick's epitaph by William Taylour.

As You are, so were Wee
And as Wee are, so shall You be.

St Werburgh's Church

This is on the site of Dublin's first theatre and a fish-and-chip shop, and is the burial place of Edward Fitzgerald, the 1798 rebellion leader, and 'Molly Malone, fishmonger'.

Shaw's birthplace

33 Synge Street
The first home of the renowned playwright, George Bernard Shaw has now been restored and has a tiny neat garden.

The young Shaw lived in this elegant Victorian home until he was ten years old.

Tailor's Guild Hall

This is the only guild hall that has survived in Dublin.

Tailor's Guild Hall

This has a musician's gallery from the 1700s where Wolfe Tone and Napper Tandy voiced their revolutionary ideas before the 1798 uprising.

Temple Bar

This area was named after Sir William Temple, a 17th century owner of the marshy land where once Augustinian friars went about their business.

Temple Bar was the last surviving part of Dublin that kept its original medieval street plan. By the 1700s it was full of brothels, pubs and vagabonds.

Trinity College

Trinity College was founded by Queen Elizabeth I in 1591–2.

Trinity College is the oldest of Dublin's three universities. (The others are University College Dublin and Dublin City University.)

A stone under the central campanile commemorates its foundation by Queen Elizabeth I on the site of the first building work. It is said that the bell rings only when another virgin walks under the campanile.

Its green lawns and cobbled quadrangles provide a calm haven in the heart of the city. Famous graduates have included Edmund Burke and Oliver Goldsmith whose statues stand outside.

Trinity College was used as the setting for the (supposedly English) university in the film with Michael Caine and Julie Walters, *Educating Rita.*

The Museum building in glorious Venetian Gothic style was designed by Benjanin Woodward in 1852.

Trinity College Library

Here can be found the Book of Durrow, an

illuminated manuscript of the Gospels which dates from about AD 675.

This is home to some 200,000 priceless books visited by about 3,000 people a day in the summer.

The entire library collection of about 3 million books is stored at another site where half a mile or so of new shelving is built each year.

Trinity College: The Old Library

The library houses the famous 8th-century *Book of Kells*, the decorated Gospel book made by Celtic monks.

Book of Kells

Whitefriar Street Carmelite Church

This is said to house the relics of Saint Valentine.

Our Lady of Dublin is a beautiful wooden statue here, believed to have been used, very irreverently, as a pig trough for a long time after the Reformation.

Museums and Galleries

Chester Beatty Library

Set up by an American mining magnate, this houses many ancient artefacts and manuscripts plus a storybook by Matisse and 1920s fashion plates from Paris.

Civic Museum

58 South William Street, Dublin 2
Its intriguing collection includes Viking artefacts and, from more recent times, Lord Nelson's head – from the statue blown up by the IRA in 1966 which once stood atop a great pillar on O'Connell Street.

Built in 1765 for the Society of Artists, this has served as a Municipal council chamber, the Court of Conscience (a doctor's court), a stable for the fire brigade and the Dáil's Supreme Court in 1919.

Collin Barracks

This fine building from the 1600s is the oldest military barracks in Europe and now houses the National Museum's decorative arts collection.

Douglas Hyde Gallery

Trinity College, Dublin
This is one of Ireland's leading contemporary art

galleries. Themed programmes include exhibitions by emerging and well-established artists and the gallery explores contemporary art, film, mixed-media, sculpture, painting and video.

The Dublin Experience

This 30-minute multi-media show takes place in the Trinity College Arts building, just across the square from the entrance to The Book of Kells.

Dublin City Gallery

This gallery of modern art includes Impressionist masterpieces by Renoir, Degas, Monet, Morisot; as well as works by contemporary Irish and International artists and the Studio of Francis Bacon, together with its entire contents of over 7,500 items.

Dublinia

A museum of history geared towards keeping children entertained while learning about the city's past. It includes a scale model of medieval Dublin.

Dublin Writers Museum

18–19 Parnell Square, Dublin 1
The Dublin Writers Museum features exhibits on

the lives and works of Dublin's literary figures such as Yeats, Shaw, Beckett, Swift and Joyce. Their books, letters and portraits are housed in a beautifully restored Georgian house.

The GAA Museum

Officially opened on 1 September, 1988, this museum commemorates and celebrates the Gaelic Athletic Association's enormous contribution to Irish sporting, cultural and social life since its foundation in 1884.

Croke Park is the home of Ireland's national games of hurling and football.

Gallery of Photography

Meeting House Square
Launched in 1978, the gallery has become Ireland's premier venue for photography and has now moved to a purpose-built space with fully fitted darkrooms in Meeting House Square.

The Guinness Storehouse

St James's Gate
This allows visitors to experience what life can be like in one of the most famous breweries in the world. Here there are exhibitions, a chance to discover all about the history of Guinness

and its advertising campaigns – plus a complimentary pint!

Heraldic Museum

Dublin Castle, Dublin 2
Here the Chief Herald used to trace your ancestral family for a fee or provide you with a coat of arms. It has a fun frieze of monkeys playing billiards.

The Irish Craft Council Gallery

Powerscourt Townhouse Centre
This offers an excellent introduction to contemporary Irish crafts.

Jewish Museum

13–14 Walworth road
This includes the reconstruction of an 1800s kitchen and a synagogue – plus information on pogroms.

The Joyce Tower

Sandycove, Co. Dublin
Devoted to the life and work of James Joyce with letters, photographs, rare first editions and personal items, this museum is housed in a Martello Tower, built to withstand invasion by Napoleon.

The Joyce Tower features in the first chapter of *Ulysses*. His character Buck Mulligam performed his ablutions on the narrow staircase that leads to the open top of the tower.

James Joyce spent a week in the tower in 1904 but left when a fellow guest seized a gun during a nightmare and shot at a row of saucepans just above his head.

Here you can see a copy of *Ulysses,* beautifully illustrated by Henri Matisse.

Museum of Modern Art

This is housed in the Royal Hospital Kilmainham that cared for military veterans and dates from 1684.

This building was modelled on Les Invalides in Paris.

The exhibits are a regularly changing collection of European works as well as Irish modern art all presented in its clean white galleries.

This museum purchases the work of living artists, but accepts loans and donations of more historical art objects with a particular emphasis on work from the 1940s onwards.

A lovely formal baroque garden has been restored in the grounds here.

National Gallery of Ireland

The collection spans some 600 years of art and includes Irish painting from the 17th century to Jack B. Yeats and works by Ireland's most important recent artists.

Italian School exhibits at the National Gallery of Ireland include gilded altarpieces and Renaissance treasures.

National Library

Kildare Street

This is home to the world's largest collection of Irish documentary material and includes books, manuscripts, newspapers, periodicals, drawings, photographs, maps and illustrated material. The Library has an ongoing programme of exhibitions and a Family History Research centre.

The National Museum

Kildare Street

The National Museum was opened in 1890 with bequests from the Royal Irish Academy, the Royal

Dublin Society and and Trinity College. Today the collections are housed in Irish Antiquities, Art and Industrial, and Natural History.

The Antiquities exhibits include the finest collection of early European Christian art including the Ardagh Chalice, the Cross of Cong and the Tara Brooch.

The National Museum of Ireland
Decorative Arts & History

Ireland's museum of decorative arts has artefacts that include weapons, jewellery, ceramics, glassware and silver, furniture, clothing, coins and currency.

The National Museum of Ireland
Natural History

This explores both world zoology (especially wildlife of Africa and Asia) and the wildlife of Ireland.

This part of the museum has a complete collection of the prehistoric giant Irish deer, known as Irish elk, long since hunted to extinction.

Many of the species on display are now rare or endangered and the museum is sometimes nicknamed the 'Dead Zoo'.

An impressive collection of animal skeletons includes whales, elephants and a giraffe.

National Print Museum

Garrison Chapel, Beggars Bush
Haddington Road, Dublin 4
This collection was launched in 1985 to save printing machinery from the 'hot metal' era before computers changed the technology so dramatically, and has exhibits associated with the history, present state and future development of the printing craft in Ireland.

The Museum was officially opened in 1996. An audio-visual show documents the old skills of printing and shows many of the Museum's machines in operation. The museum also has a vast array of woodblocks and half-tone engravings.

Old Jameson Distillery

This offers a guided tour and an audio-visual presentation on the distilling of Irish whiskey plus information on the 1924 World Exhibition.

Old Jameson Distillery: The Smithfield Chimney

A 53 metre (175 feet) chimney from the distillery now acts as 360-degree skyline observatory with an external glass elevator.

The Oriel Gallery

Clare Street

There are many fine 20th-century works on sale.

Original Print Gallery

4 Temple Bar

A showcase for printmakers and with many folders of both Irish and International works.

Rubicon Gallery

Initiated in 1990 by Josephine Kelliher and Peter McKenna, with the exhibition space set up at

10 Saint Stephens Green in 1995, the gallery's core objective is to enable living artists to realise important projects. Today the gallery works with international artists in all media to present many exhibitions.

The Solomon Gallery

Powerscourt Townhouse
Exhibits the work of contemporary Irish artists.

Temple Bar Gallery

This gallery exhibits the work of up to 40 resident artists.

Trinity College and The Book of Kells

The ancient religious manuscript, possibly dating from the 11th century, was beautifully illuminated by the scholars of the day.

The Book of Kells exhibition leads on into the College's Old Library with its fine Long Room and row upon row of antique books.

Waterways Visitor centre

Here you can discover much about Dublin's intricate network of canals and waterways.

Shops and markets

The main shopping areas are Nassau Street, Grafton Street, St. Stephen's Green, Temple Bar, O'Connell Street and Henry Street.

Grafton Street

Grafton Street is a busy hub of cafés, restaurants and department stores. Here buskers not only play music but also recite poetry. All the main department stores are on Grafton Street, as well as branches of larger chain stores such as Marks and Spencers, HMV and The Body Shop.

The Ilac Centre in Grafton Street is a northside shopping complex built in the 1980s. Its boutiques, gift-shops and fast food restaurants offers a hotchpotch of souvenirs, Irish craft and interesting things to eat. Here, for example, Dunnes Stores sells Irish products and food.

St Ilac's even provides a library and a small chapel.

The St Stephen's Green shopping centre

This is the largest shopping mall in Dublin. Here you can buy – and eat – just about anything.

The Powerscourt Townhouse

In Clarendon Street this small mall specialises in restaurants, crafts, jewellery and clothes stores.

The Royal Hibernian Way

This is a small shopping mall with very exclusive clothes shops. It connects Lemon Street with Dawson Street and has an eclectic collection of shops and a good wine bar, Cocoon, owned by former Formula 1 racing driver Eddie Irivine.

Francis Street, Dublin 7

This is a famous 'antique highway' with many art and antique stores plus Wraptures that stocks fine-papers – papyrus, bark, glitter, embroidered gift wrap, hand-marbled and multi-coloured chrome papers, plus pens, quills, pencils, inks, paper weights, rubber stamps, embossing powders, ink pads, handmade waxes, seals and ribbons.

Mother Redcap's Market

One of Dublin's best markets, it is in Back Lane (opposite Christchurch Cathedral). Here stalls sell clothes, music, books, antiques, cakes and cheeses.

Bachelors Walk and Ormond Quay on the Liffey

Today there are antique bargains galore here. On 26 July, 1914, a unit of the Kings Own Scottish Borders opened fire on an unarmed group of

Dublin civilians at Bachelors Walk, wounding 37 and killing 4. No one was courtmartialled; the official explanation was that the commanding officer's orders had been misinterpreted.

Bookshops

Dublin has many fine bookshops, covering general and specialist books, both new and second-hand. Some of the best include Waterstones and Hodges Figgis (of *Ulysses* fame), on Dawson Street, both of which have special Irish interest sections.

Fred Hanna in Nassau Street

Fred Hanna sells both new and second-hand books, posters and old postcards in a lovely topsy-turvy shop.

International Books, on South Frederick Street

International Books specialises in books on languages with course books, novels, audio courses, reference books and teacher resources.

The Irish Film Centre in Estate Street

This is devoted to books on cinema and television.

Eason's on Lower O'Connell Street

Eason's is a huge general bookshop with vast periodical and international press sections and a raised corner for coffee and lunch.

The Winding Stair on Ormond Quay

The Winding Stair is a popular second-hand bookshop with a labyrinth of shelving plus a café.

Chocolates!

Exquisite Belgian hand-made chocolates are on sale in the Royal Hibernian Way and in Mary

Street. Irish hand-made chocolates are available at Butlers Irish Chocolates in Grafton Street.

Fine crystal

Exquisite Waterford, Cavan, Galway, Tipperary and Tyrone crystal can be bought in many Dublin stores including the House of Ireland.

Temple Bar Food Market

This weekly market is great to visit for shoppers who enjoy fine cuisine, organic produce and fresh ingredients. Held at Meeting House Square every Saturday, it is a veritable gourmet's paradise offering everything from fresh Atlantic oysters, organic vegetables, crêpes, cheese, and chutneys to homemade breads.

New Square

Every Sunday this hosts a second-hand book fair with many vintage paperback classics.

Cows Lane Fashion and Design Market

Cows Lane sells clothes by talented new designers with all the latest trends and innovative designs on sale. This fashion extravaganza is open every Saturday in the old Temple Bar area.

Claudio Meneses Wines

Claudio Meneses from Brazil stocks a wide and extensive range of wines from around the world. These include the best-priced Bollinger Champagne in Ireland.

CoCo Markets

This is a new initiative organised on behalf of Dún Laoghaire Rathdown County Council. Three gourmet artisan markets take place in Dalkey on Fridays, Marlay Park on Saturdays and Dún Laoghaire People's Park on Sundays.

Every stallholder at the CoCo markets is thoroughly vetted to ensure only 100% wholesome ingredients and organic produce are sold. The aim is to provide all sorts of fresh fruit and vegetables, cheeses, olives and bakery goods plus a range of smoked vegan products.

George's Street Arcade

Here some exotic gift options are sold in a charming Victorian building. A wide range of shops and stalls is nearby.

New Moon

A jewellery shop that specialises in intricate silver jewellery but also stocks ethnic crafts from the Far East, such as wooden jewellery boxes from Indonesia, stone pendants or Buddhas made of wood.

Barry Doyle Design Jewellers

Above George's Street Arcade
Exquisite pieces of jewellery are handmade and include cuff-links with semi-precious stones, silver bracelets and a selection of designer rings.

Temple Bar Book Market

This runs every Saturday from 10am-5.30pm. Some real gems in literature and the arts may be found here.

The Dublin Food Co-op

Saint Andrew Centre, Pearse Street, Dublin 2
Open every Saturday: over a thousand members specialise in organic food plus flour, oat flakes, pasta, sea food and vegetables. The produce is largely Irish-produced. The co-op was set up in 1983 during a campaign to stop a nuclear power station being built at Carnsore Point in Wexford.

Gallic Kitchen

Meeting House Square
Gallic Kitchen produce high quality, homemade food and sell their wares from a retail outlet in Francis Street and from market stalls in Temple Bar on Saturdays. There is a delicious range of pastries, quiches, and desserts, jars of their own jam, relish and chutney.

Lara Lu's food stall

This offers a wide range of goodies such as elegant boxes of chocolates and Italian cakes and biscuits – as well as sandwiches, soups, stews and coffees.

Hotels, restaurants and cafés

Bewley's Coffee House

Bewley's was established around 1840 in Dublin by one Joshua Bewley of a Quaker family. Here for years people could relax and read a newspaper as well as drinking coffee but now some branches trade just as a tea and coffee merchants.

Famous writers have frequented Bewley's and authors have been known to write some parts of their manuscripts in this cosy atmosphere, sipping the fine tea, coffees or hot chocolate with mallow.

The best known branch of Bewley's is in Grafton Street where there is also a small museum about

the history of Bewley's coffee houses.
In the 1920s Bewleys became caught up in the Tutankhamun fever and its façade is covered with mosaics of Egyptian symbols. It is worth pausing here at number 78 to admire them.

The Clarence Hotel

This is owned by the famous pop group, U2.

Captain America's

Grafton Street
Not just burger and chips, this place doubles as a rock 'n 'roll museum, with the first drum kit that

Larry Mullen of U2 ever had, a guitar from The Edge, a Rickenbacker signed by all four members of R.E.M., signed Rolling Stones ephemera and a cami-top belonging to Cindy Crawford.

Gallagher's Boxty House

Temple Bar
Keenly priced traditional fare includes boxty, their famous potato pancakes, stuffed with various fillings. This place is very popular and very good – and they do serve food other than boxty!

Kitty Kaboodle's

Here each table is furnished with a paper tablecloth and a pot of crayons for mealtime doodles. The walls are festooned with the resulting artwork.

Dublin wit

Considering its relatively small size, Ireland has made a disproportionate contribution to world literature and drama, over some 400 years or so.

The works that are best known outside the country are in English, but Irish Gaelic also has a significant body of written literature, both ancient and recent, in addition to a strong oral tradition of legends and poetry. The city played a leading role in the revival of Irish language and literature of the late 19th and early 20th centuries.

Here follows a selection of quotes from the city's famous, especially its literary figures.

Trinity College, founded in 1591, has seen the graduation of numerous famous authors including Jonathan Swift, Oliver Goldsmith and Oscar Wilde.

Brendan Behan commented . . .

Shakespeare said pretty well everything and what he left out, James Joyce . . . put in.

James Connolly said of Irish authors . . .

The Irishman in English literature may be said to have been born with an apology in his mouth.

Samuel Lover 1797–1868 a Dublin-born Irish song-writer, painter and novelist wrote . . .

When once the itch of literature comes over a man, nothing can cure it but the scratching of a pen.

Samuel Beckett 1906–1989

Samuel Beckett was born in Dublin and lectured at Trinity College there. He won the Nobel Prize for Literature in 1969 and is probably best known for his play *Waiting for Godot* (1952).

We are all born mad. Some remain so.

Words are all we have.

We lose our hair, our teeth! Our bloom, our ideals.

If I had the use of my body, I would throw it out the window.

Try Again. Fail again. Fail better.

Birth was the death of him.

Nothing is funnier than unhappiness. . . .

Dublin university contains the cream of Ireland: Rich and thick.

. . . grow gently old down all the unchanging days, and die one day like any other day, only shorter.

Personally I have no bone to pick with graveyards.

Brendan Behan 1923–1964

Brendan Francis Behan was a most successful poet, short-story writer, novelist and playwright who wrote in both English and Irish (in Gaeilge, a Goidelic language spoken in Ireland). He was a committed Irish Republican and a member of the Irish Republican Army.

Renee McCall of the *Daily Express* on the passing

of Brendan Behan at the age of 41 said . . ..

Too young to die. Too drunk to live

Brendan Behan's last words were to several nuns standing over his bed . . .

God bless you, may your sons all be bishops.

Critics are like eunuchs in a harem; they know how it's done, they've seen it done every day, but they're unable to do it themselves.

I am a drinker with writing problems.

If it was raining soup, the Irish would go out with forks.

The big difference between sex for money and sex for free is that sex for money usually costs a lot less.

One drink is too many for me and a thousand not enough.

The most important things to do in the world are to get something to eat, something to drink and somebody to love you.

There is no such thing as bad publicity except your own obituary.

I saw a notice which said, 'Drink Canada Dry' and I've just started.

Maeve Binchy 1940 –

Irish columnist, short story writer and novelist

It wasn't every day that you overheard a conversation that covered lies, virginity, knickers and God-all-bloody-mighty. Dublin was changing.

"I'm not complaining," Hilary said, even though she rarely did anything but complain, "But it does seem an odd way for God to have sorted out the whole business of continuing the human race. Wouldn't

you think He would have arranged something much more sensible, like people going to an agency and giving proof that they could bring up a child properly, instead of teenagers getting pregnant from gropings in the bicycle sheds."

It was one of those houses that just put out its arms and hugged you.

It did old people good to see a baby; it made them think there was some continuity in life.

Dion Boucicault 1820–1890

This playwright, author and theatre manager was

born in Dublin; he wrote or adapted about 130 plays.

Men talk of killing time, while time quietly kills them.

I wish Adam had died with all the ribs in his body.

Edmund Burke 1729–1797

Stateman and philospher born in Dublin and educated at Trinity College.

Ambition can creep as well as soar.

We must not always judge of the generality of the opinion by the noise of the acclamation.

Flattery corrupts both the receiver and the giver.

Nothing turns out to be so oppressive and unjust as a feeble government.

Laws, like houses, lean on one another.

He that wrestles with us strengthens our nerves, and sharpens our skill.

I have never yet seen any plan which has not been mended by the observations of those who were much inferior in understanding to the person who took the lead in the business.

A state without the means of some change is without the means of its conservation.

People will not look forward to posterity, who never look backward to their ancestors.

Kings will be tyrants from policy, when subjects are rebels from principle.

The arrogance of age must submit to be taught by youth.

George Farquhar 1677–1707

This poet and dramatist studied at Trinity College and became an actor in Dublin before joining the army. His most famous works are *The Recruiting Officer* (1706) and *The Beaux Stratagem* (1707).

There is no scandal like rags, nor any crime so shameful as poverty.

How a little love and good company improves a woman!

We have heads to get money, and hearts to spend it.

I have fed purely upon ale; I have eat my ale, drank my ale, and I always sleep upon ale.

Observe this, that tho a woman swear, forswear, lie, dissemble, back-bite, be proud, vain, malicious, anything, if she secures the main chance, she's still virtuous.

Necessity, the mother of invention.

Those who know the least obey the best.

Oliver Goldsmith 1728–1774

Playwright, novelist and poet who studied at

Dublin, he wrote *The Vicar of Wakefield* (1766),
The Deserted Village (1770) and
She Stoops to Conquer (1773)

Be not affronted at a joke. If one throw salt at thee, thou wilt receive no harm, unless thou art raw.

Every absurdity has a champion to defend it.

Friendship is a disinterested commerce between equals; love, an abject intercourse between tyrants and slaves.

Hope is such a bait, it covers any hook.

Let schoolmasters puzzle their brain,
With grammar, and nonsense, and learning,
Good liquor, I stoutly maintain,
Gives genius a better discerning.

Man wants but little here below, nor wants that little long.

Our greatest glory consists not in never failing, but in rising every time we fall.

People seldom improve when they have no other model but themselves to copy.

The very pink of perfection.

Where wealth accumulates, men decay.

You can preach a better sermon with your life than with your lips.

James Joyce 1882–1941

This famous author was born in Dublin and studied at University College there.
His most famous works include *Ulysses* (1904), based on a single day in Dublin, *Dubliners* (1914), *A Portrait of the Artist as a Young Man* (1916) and *Finnegans Wake* (1939).

Ireland is the old sow that eats her farrow.

James Joyce

Christopher Columbus, as everyone knows, is honored by posterity because he was the last to discover America.

I am tomorrow, or some future day,
what I establish today.
I am today what I established yesterday
or some previous day.

I shall write a book some day about the appropriateness of names. Geoffrey Chaucer has a ribald ring . . . and Shelley was very Percy and very Bysshe.

Mistakes are the portals of discovery.

No pen, no ink, no table, no room, no time, no quiet, no inclination.

The actions of men are the best interpreters of their thoughts.

Patrick Kavanagh 1904–1967

This son of a farmer and cobbler became a renowned poet. In 1931 he walked to Dublin to meet George Russell and Patrick O'Connor. Soon his poetry met with wide acclaim

What appears in newspapers is often new but seldom true.

A man is original when he speaks the truth that has always been known to all good men.

Joseph Sheridan Le Fanu 1814–1873

Born in Dublin, journalist, newspaper proprietor and writer, Le Fanu studied at Trinity College and was called to the bar in 1839.
He wrote *The House by the Churchyard* in 1863 and *Uncle Silas* in 1864 and also penned a vampire novella, *Carmilla*. Richard Brinsley Sheridan was Le Fanu's great-uncle.

Perhaps other souls than human are sometimes born into the world, and clothed in flesh.

Nothing is more mysterious than the spread of rumour. It is like a vial poured on the air. It travels, like an epidemic, on the sightless currents of the atmosphere . . .

. . . trifles are always remembered after the catastrophe.

Knowledge is power – and power of one sort or another is the secret lust of human souls . . .

Iris Murdoch 1919–1999

A novelist and philospher born in Dublin, Dame Iris Murdoch began her novel writing as a hobby and went on to prove a most prolific and highly successful writer

Bereavement is a darkness impenetrable to the imagination of the unbereaved.

Perhaps misguided moral passion is better than confused indifference.

A bad review is even less important than whether it is raining in Patagonia.

Human affairs are not serious, but they have to be taken seriously.

Falling out of love is chiefly a matter of forgetting how charming someone is.

We shall be better prepared for the future if we see how terrible, how doomed the present is.

There is no substitute for the comfort supplied by the utterly taken-for-granted relationship.

I think being a woman is like being Irish. . . .
Everyone says you're important and nice,
but you take second place all the same.

Writing is like getting married. One should never commit oneself until one is amazed at one's luck.

Edna O'Brien, 1936

Edna O'Brian studied pharmacy in Dublin before becoming a writer of short stories and a journalist.

My hand does the work and I don't have to think;
in fact, were I to think, it would stop the flow.
It's like a dam in the brain that bursts.

The vote means nothing to women.
We should be armed.

When anyone asks me about the Irish character, I say . . . look at the trees. Maimed, stark and misshapen, but ferociously tenacious.

Writing is like carrying a foetus.

Sean O'Casey, 1880–1964

His plays include *The Shadow of a Gunman* (1923), *Juno and the Paycock* (1924) and *The Plough and the Stars* (1926) all staged at The Abbey Theatre, the last causing a riot after which he left Ireland.

. . . a rich man makes the law that hallows and hollows his own life.

A lament in one ear, maybe, but always a song in the other.

The military mind is indeed a menace. Old-fashioned futurity that sees only men fighting and dying in smoke and fire; hears nothing more civilized than a cannonade; scents nothing but the stink of battle-wounds and blood.

What time has been wasted during man's destiny in the struggle to decide what man's next world will be like! The keener the effort to find out, the less he knew about the present one he lived in.

Liam O'Flaherty 1896–1984

This author was born in Cork but studied at University College, Dublin, and depicts the city in short stories and novels such as *The Informer* (a film version was made by his cousin John Ford). His works have realism and powerful drama. Although a native speaker of Irish, he wrote mostly in English.

I was born on a storm-swept rock and hate the soft growth of sunbaked lands where there is no frost in men's bones.

The only things a creative artist can be opposed to are ugliness and injustice.

George Russell 1867–1935

A critic, poet, painter and mystical writer: Russell's family moved from County Armagh to Dublin when he was 11. He started working as a draper there but later became editor of both *The Irish Homestead* and *The Irish Statesman*. He met the young James Joyce in 1902 and appears as a character in Joyce's *Ulysses*.

Ah, to think how thin the veil that lies
Between the pain of hell and Paradise.

Forgive me, Spirit of my spirit, for this, that I have found it easier to read the mystery told in tears and understood Thee better in sorrow than in joy.

Our hearts were drunk with a beauty
Our eyes could never see.

Seek on earth what you have found in heaven.

Twilight, a timid fawn, went glimmering by
And Night, the dark-blue hunter, followed fast.

You can't evoke great spirits
and eat plums at the same time.

George Bernard Shaw 1856–1950

Shaw was born in Dublin and found his first employment in an office there. He moved to London in 1876 where he beacme famous for his witty and thought-provoking plays that include *Arms and the Man* and *Saint Joan*. He received the Nobel prize for literature in 1925.

Marriage is popular because it combines the maximum of temptation with the maximum of opportunity.

All great truths begin as blasphemies.

George Bernard Shaw

You see things; and you say, "Why?"
But I dream things that never were;
and I say, "Why not?"

On marriage . . .

If you must hold yourself up to your children as an object lesson, hold yourself up as a warning and not an example.

When two people are under the influence of the most violent, most insane, most delusive, and most transient of passions, they are required to swear that they will remain in that excited, abnormal, and exhausting condition continuously until death do them part.

There are no secrets better kept than the secrets that everybody guesses.

If you cannot get rid of the family skeleton you might as well make it dance.

He knows nothing and thinks he knows everything. That points clearly to a political career.

Do you know what a pessimist is?
A man who thinks everybody as nasty as himself, and hates them for it.

Alcohol is the anæsthesia by which we endure the operation of life.

It is dangerous to be sincere unless you are also stupid.

Democracy is a device that insures we shall be governed no better than we deserve.

I often quote myself; it adds spice to my conversation.

There is no satisfaction in hanging a man who does not object to it.

A life spent making mistakes is not only more honorable, but more useful than a life spent doing nothing.

He who can, does.
He who cannot, teaches.

Assassination is the extreme form of censorship.

Richard Brinsley Sheridan 1751–1816

The author of *The Rivals* and *The School for Scandal,* who was born in Dublin, eloped with a singer and fought a duel on her account.

Fertilizer does no good in a heap, but a little spread around works miracles all over.

He is the very pineapple of politeness!

. . . the question actors most often get asked is how they can bear saying the same things over and over again, night after night, but God knows the answer to that is, don't we all anyway; might as well get paid for it.

Conscience has no more to do with gallantry than it has with politics.

Won't you come into the garden? I would like my roses to see you.

Pity those who nature abuses;
never those who abuse nature.

The surest way to fail is not to determine to succeed.

There's no possibility of being witty
without a little ill-nature.

Those that vow the most are the least sincere.

Bram Stoker 1847–1912

Bram Stoker was born near Dublin and, a sick child, was virtually bedridden until aged seven but later became an athlete and at Trinity College, Dublin, was named University Athlete. He wrote several short stories, novels and essays; his most famous work, *Dracula,* was published in 1897.

Despair has its own calms.

No man knows till he has suffered from the night how sweet and dear to his heart and eye the morning can be.

For life be, after all, only a waitin' for somethin' else than what we're doin', and death be all that we can rightly depend on.

We learn from failure, not from success!

How blessed are some people, whose lives have no fears, no dreads, to whom sleep is a blessing that comes nightly.

I have tried to keep an open mind, and it is not the ordinary things of life that could close it, but the strange things, the extraordinary things. . .

We are all drifting reefwards now, and faith is our only anchor.

Jonathan Swift 1667–1745

Clergyman, author and satirist, Swift is most famous for his satire, *Gulliver's Travels* but was also the dean of St Patrick's Cathedral in Dublin and identified closely with Irish causes.

Vision is the art of seeing what is invisible to others.

Jonathan Swift

How is it possible to expect mankind to take advice when they will not so much as take warning?

Happiness is a perpetual possession of being well-deceived.

Two women seldom grow intimate but at the expense of a third person.

There are few wild beasts more to be dreaded than a talking man having nothing to say.

There's none so blind as they that won't see.

May you live all the days of your life.

A wise man should have money in his head,
but not in his heart.

John Millington Synge 1871–1909

Born in Dublin, Synge studied at Trinity College. He met William Butler Yeats in Paris and then returned to Dublin to write *152* and plays such as *In the Shadow of the Glen,* (1903), *Riders to the Sea* (1904), *The Well of the Saints* (1905) and, most famously, *The Playboy of the Western World* (1907).

There is no language like the Irish
for soothing and quieting.

If one could only teach the English how to talk,
and the Irish how to listen,
society would be quite civilized.

A man who is not afraid of the sea
will soon be drownded.

I'm a good scholar when it comes to reading
but a blotting kind of writer
when you give me a pen.

Oscar Wilde 1854–1900

Born in Dublin and a graduate of Trinity College, he became famous for his sparkling wit and his highly successful plays such as *The Importance of being Earnest* and *Lady Windermere's Fan*. Imprisoned for homosexual activities, he died an exile in Paris.

Art never expresses anything but itself.

It is very vulgar to talk like a dentist,
when one isn't a dentist.
It produces a false impression.

Oscar Wilde

On an occasion of this kind, it becomes more than a moral duty to speak one's mind. It becomes a pleasure.

Anyone can be good in the country.

Many a woman has a past, but I am told that she has at least a dozen, and that they all fit.

A man cannot be too careful in the choice of his enemies.

It is better to be beautiful than to be good. But . . . it is better to be good than to be ugly.

A thing is not necessarily true
because a man dies for it.

Yet each man kills the thing he loves,
By each let this be heard,
Some do it with a bitter look,
Some with a flattering word,
The coward does it with a kiss,
The brave man with a sword!
(The Ballad of Reading Gaol)

He hasn't an enemy in the world,
and none of his friends like him.

Ah! Don't say that you agree with me. When people agree with me I always feel that I must be wrong.

As long as war is regarded as wicked, it will always have its fascination. When it is looked upon as vulgar, it will cease to be popular.

A little sincerity is a dangerous thing, and a great deal of it is absolutely fatal.

At New York customs

I have nothing to declare except my genius.

They say . . . that when good Americans die they go to Paris.

Indeed? And when bad Americans die,
where do they go to?
Oh, they go to America.

Democracy means simply the bludgeoning of the people by the people for the people.

Really, if the lower orders don't set us a good example, what on earth is the use of them?

Experience is the name
everyone gives to their mistakes.

We are all in the gutter but some of us
are looking at the stars.

I can resist everything except temptation.

The truth is rarely pure, and never simple.

Work is the curse of the drinking classes.

William Butler Yeats 1865–1939

This poet and playwright was born near Dublin and educated both here and in London. A leader of the Irish Literary Revival, his numerous plays include *The Land of Heart's Desire* and he received the Nobel Prize for Literature in 1923 and was a Senator of the Irish Free State 1922–28.

William Butler Yeats

Of our conflicts with others we make rhetoric;
of our conflicts with ourselves we make poetry.

The innocent and the beautiful
Have no enemy but time.

Irish poets, learn your trade,
Sing whatever is well made,
Scorn the sort now growing up
All out of shape from toe to top

The intellect of man is forced to choose
perfection of the life, or of the work.

Only God, my dear,
Could love you for yourself alone
And not your yellow hair.

We taste and feel and see the truth.
We do not reason ourselves into it.

Education is not the filling of a pail,
but the lighting of a fire.

Other famous people born in Dublin

Dubliners are individuals, many giving full expression to their Irish wit, artistic flair or political fire. As British prime minister Winston Churchill once said:

We have always found the Irish a bit odd.
They refuse to be English.

Here are just a few of them:

Dave Allen 1936–2005

Born in Tallaght, Dublin, the son of Cully Tynan O'Mahoney, managing editor of the *Irish Times*, Dave Allen went on to become a famous comedian and television star and in 1967 won the Variety Club's ITV Personality of the Year Award.

Francis Bacon 1909–1992

Painter, atheist, gambler and bon vivant, Bacon was born in a Lower Baggot Street nursing home in Dublin. He was a sickly child, with asthma, but grew up to be a renowned artist with a prolific output.

Thomas John Barnardo 1845–1905

This founder of homes for destitute children began the foundation of the homes in 1867 and carried on the good work until his death – by which time nearly 60,000 children had been rescued, trained and given a place in life.

Brian Boru 941–1014

This High King of Ireland successfully drove the Viking invaders out of Ireland in the Battle of Clontarf. His name actually means tax collector; kings traditionally had the right to collect taxes.

Christy Brown 1932

This disabled writer and painter painted and typed, using only his right foot. His autobiography *My Left Foot* was made into a movie in 1989.

Gay Byrne 1934

Broadcaster Gabriel Mary Byrne was the man who introduced the Beatles on their first television appearance. He also hosted one of the longest-running television chat shows in the world, *The Late Late Show.*

Edward Carson 1854–1935

This orator, politician and founder of modern Unionism was born in Harcourt Street in Dublin and studied law at Trinity College.

Bill Cullen 1942

This entrepreneur grew up in Dublin in the tough inner city slums of Summerhill. One of fourteen children, he was a street seller from the age of six and left school at thirteen.

Bill Cullen progressed from selling dolls and cinema tickets on street corners to head a company with a turnover of more than 250 million pounds and he is now one of the richest men in Ireland.

Ronnie Drew 1934

Ronnie Drew was born and reared in Dún Laoghaire on the coast of south County Dublin.

This lead vocalist and guitar player founded the Dubliners as the Ronnie Drew Folk Group in 1962.

Bob Geldof 1954

From Laoghaire, County Dublin, this Irish singer, songwriter, actor, political activist and rock star went on to win world acclaim for his efforts to get relief aid for Africa

William Rowan Hamilton 1805–65

This mathematician, physicist and astronomer was the inventor of quaternions, which he discovered in 1843.

William Rowan Hamilton chiseled one particularly good equation onto a bridge over the Royal Canal and received the probation act as a result.

Alfred Harmsworth, 1st Viscount Northcliffe
1865–1922

This powerful and influential newspaper magnate
established the *Daily Mail* in 1896
founded the *Daily Mirror* in 1903
and purchased *The Times* in 1908.

Paul David Hewson (Bono) 1960

This Dublin rock star (nicknamed Bono Vox) is the lead singer of the renowned Irish rock band, U2.

Luke Kelly 1940–1984

This folksinger, vocalist and 5-string banjo player, a member of the Dubliners from 1962–1963 and 1964–1984, has a park and bridge named after him.

Phil Lynott 1949–1986

Philip Parris Lynott was the lead singer and bass player with Thin Lizzy, the Irish rock band.

Philip was brought up in Crumlin, Dublin, by his grandmother.

Diarmuid McMurrough 1110–1171

This Irish king of Leinster invited the Normans into Ireland in 1169 – including Norman warrior 'Strongbow' – to sort out a few feuds. This led to 800 years of British imperial domination.

Sinead O'Connor 1966

This petite singer and songwriter was named after Sinéad de Valera, the wife of Irish President Eamon de Valera. She has been one of the most distinctive and controversial pop music stars of the 1990s.

Maureen O'Hara 1920-

Actress and movie star Maureen O'Hara was once named one of the world's most beautiful women. She often worked with John Ford and John Wayne and starred in many movies, including *How Green Was My Valley*. This famous redhead has a star on the Hollywood Walk of Fame.

Theobald Wolf Tone 1663–1798

Revolutionary and leading figure in the Irish

Independent movement: the son of a coachmaker, he was born on St Bride's Street, just behind Dublin castle. He eloped with a girl of sixteen, read law in London and Dublin and was called to the Irish bar in 1789. He wrote in 1791 a remarkable essay – of which 10,000 copies were said to have been sold.

There are many more, as follows:

Sara Allgood 1883–1950

Actress

Eamon Andrews 1922–1987

Television host and presenter

Michael William Balfe 1808-1870

Composer

George Barret 1732–1784

Artist

Issac Bickerstaffe 1735–1812

Playwright

Seoirse Bodley 1933

Composer

Eavan Boland 1944

Poet

Dermot Bolger 1959

Writer

Elizabeth Bowen 1899-1973

Writer

Sean Bodley 1933

Composer

Brian Boydell 1917-2000

Musician

Gabriel Byrne 1950-

Actor

Liam Cosgrave 1920

Former Taoiseach

John A Costello 1891-1976

Taioseach

Michael Craig-Martin 1941

Artist

Gemma Craven 1950-

Actress and singer

Keith Duffy 1974

Singer

Ronald Dunlop 1894-1973

Artist

Paul Durcan 1944

Poet

Colin Farrell 1976

Actor

John Field 1782-1837

Composer

Garrett Fitzgerald 1926

Former Taoiseach

John Henry Foley 1818-1874

Sculptor

Stanhope Alexander Frobes 1857-1947

Artist

Brenda Fricker 1945

Actress

Brendan Gleeson 1955

Actor

Oliver Gogarty 1878–1957

Poet

Eamon Grennan 1941

Poet

Sir Richard Griffith 1784–1878

Geologist

Victor Herbert 1859–1924

Composer

Thomas Hickey 1741–1824

Artist

Evie Hone 1894–1955

Artist

Rex Ingram 1893–1960

Film Director

Mainie Jellett 1897–1944

Artist

Jennifer Johnston 1930

Writer

Ronan Keating 1977

Singer

Thomas Kinsella 1928-

Poet

Sean Lemass 1899–1971

Taioseach

Denis MacCarthy 1817–1882

Writer

Donagh MacDonagh 1912–1968

Writer

Niall MacGinnis 1913–1978

Actor

Colum McCann 1965

Writer

John McGahern 1934

Writer

Colm Meaney 1953

Actor

Thomas Moore 1779–1852

Poet

Mary Morrisy 1957

Writer

Richard Moynan 1856–1906

Artist

Ann Murray 1949

Singer

James Musspratt 1793–1886

Chemist

Sinead O'Connor 1966

Singer/songwriter

Eimar O'Duffy 1893-1935

Writer

Sean O'Faolain 1900-1991

Writer

Sean O'Kelly 1882–1966

Former President

Tony O'Reilly 1936

Rugby player

Milo O'Shea 1926

Actor

Richard Oldham 1858–1936

Geologist

Walter Osborne 1859–1903

Artist

Thomas Parnell 1679–1718

Poet

Patrick Henry Pearse 1879–1916

Poet

James Plunkett 1920–2003

Writer

Daniel Pollen 1813–1896

Prime Minister of New Zealand

Albert Power 1882–1945

Sculptor

Glenn Quinn 1970–2002

Actor

Kevin Roche 1922-

Architect

Jonathan Rhys Meyers 1977

Actor

Sean Scully 1945

Artist

Sir Martin Archer Shee 1769–1850

Artist

Henry Smith 1826–1883

Mathematician

Thomas Southerne 1660–1746

Playwright

Sir Richard Steele 1672–1729

Writer

James Stephens 1882–1950

Poet

Mary Swanzy 1882–1978

Artist

James Napper Tandy 1740–1803

Patriot

Katharine Tynan 1861–1931

Poet

Dublin pubs

Pubs are as much a part of life in Dublin as street cafés are in Paris. Often a legendary 'craic' with Irish music, singing and friendly people will add to the warm atmosphere.

Smoking has been banned in pubs in the Irish Republic since March 2004. If customers are caught smoking in pubs, restaurants and other enclosed workplaces, proprietors face fines of up to 3,000 Euros (£2,000).

Some bars in the capital Dublin have set up wall-mounted ash-trays and heated outdoor areas to enable smokers to smoke outside.

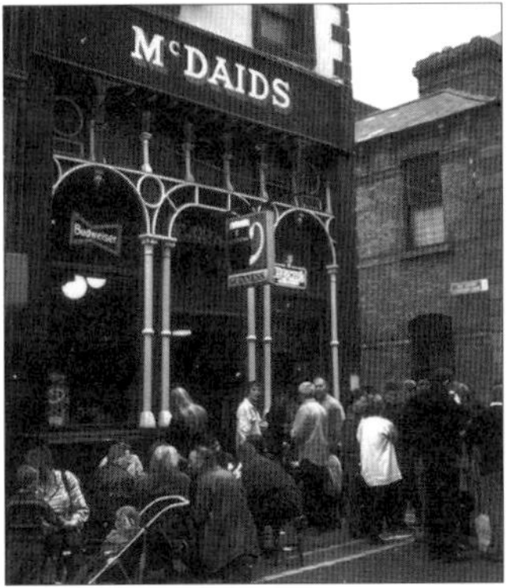

There are countless pubs in the city.
One James Joyce character said that that it would be a good puzzle to try and cross Dublin without passing one.

A study of over 80 bar staff and 40 pubs, undertaken by doctors at Trinity College, Dublin, measured pollution levels before and after the smoking ban. The level of harmful particles had been reduced by 70% while the lungs of the barmen showed a 30% increase in their performance.

There are countless pubs and bars in Dublin City, depending upon whom you believe!
600, some will tell you.
To be sure, it's more than a 1000 now,
another 'expert' will profess.

The smoking ban will not apply in hotel rooms,

prisons, nursing homes and psychiatric hospitals.

In the famous novel, *Ulysses,* by James Joyce, Leopold Bloom commented that it would be a good puzzle to try and cross Dublin without passing a pub.

Abbey Tavern

Abbey Street, Howth

Abbey Tavern is an authentic 16th-century tavern and restaurant with open turf fires and traditional, lively Irish ballad music, with fiddles, pipes, tin whistles, and 'bones' plus singing and dancing.

The Brazen Head

20 Lower Bridge Street
The Brazen Head is Dublin's oldest pub, as its swinging, varnished sign declares. It dates from 1198. The walls of the former coaching inn lean and list along with its more inebriated occupants. There are peat fires and musicians playing against walls filled with etchings and prints of the 18th-century Irish nationalist, Robert Emmet. Muskets and sabres hang from the ceiling.

A sign in The Brazen Head reads, 'Reality is an hallucination caused by lack of alcohol'.

The Cellar Bar in the Merrion Hotel

Upper Merrion Street

This bar serves its customers in the original 18th-century wine vaults with bare bricked walls and vaulted ceilings set underneath the Georgian town houses in the street above.

Davy Byrne's

Davy Byrne's has 1930s-style decor and was immortalised by James Joyce in *Ulysses* who wrote: *He entered Davy Byrne's. Moral pub. He doesn't chat. Stands a drink now and then.*

Barmen may still be referred to as curates in Davy Byrne's bar, just as in James Joyce's day. They abide by the 'Holy Hour' of 2:30pm to 4pm on Sunday afternoons, when pubs close so that both barmen and their drinking fellows can race home for family dinner.

Doheny & Nesbitts

Doheny & Nesbitts is one of Dublin's oldest drinking emporiums. This well-preserved Victorian pub has a fine bar collection of tankards, oak casks, and pump handles. Classic Dublin pub partitions, made of carved wood and etched glass, divide the long, waxed, polished bar.

Johnnie Fox's

Johnnie Fox's Pub, set in Glencullen in the Dublin mountains, claims to be the 'highest pub in Ireland' and is one of its oldest. It has live entertainment every night with Celtic music and dancing.

Kavanagh's

Kavanagh's in north Dublin is set by the entrance gate to the old Glasnevin Cemetery, hence its nickname 'The Gravedigger's'. The pub provided a vantage point for watching funerals pass, including Charles Stewart Parnell, Eamon De Valera, and probably Daniel O'Connell.

The Kavanagh family have owned Kavanagh's pub since 1833. When the cemetery gate was closed in 1879, the gravediggers knocked with their shovels on the wall of the pub and the Kavanaghs would pass drinks through the bars of the gate but any diggers caught drinking were sacked.

Left Bank Bar

The trendy late night Left Bank Bar (18/21 Anglesea Street, Temple Bar), on Dublin's Bohemian left bank, is set in a building that was once part of the Central Bank of Ireland.

Lynch's

Lynch's (Thomas Street) has its name in Gaelic over the entrance; P.O. Loingsigh – Patrick Lynch. There has been many a Patrick Lynch behind the bar for generations.

Just outside the door, Emmet led his revolutionists along the alley to their arms cache.

Lynch's pub was once a meeting place for the old Irish Republican Army and has been nicknamed The Gunman's.

McDaid's

McDaid's (Harry Street) is a famous literary pub and was the old haunt of Brendan Behan. McDaid's became the centre of a new generation of writers in the 1940s and 1950s and was also the one-time haunt of Patrick Kavanagh, Flann O'Brien, J.P. Donleavy and Liam O'Flaherty.

Brendan Behan may have based some of his characters in *The Hostage* and *Borstal Boy* on the publicans he met at McDaid's. Donleavy's main character in *The Ginger Man* was supposedly based on Ganor Christ, a regular at McDaid's.

Mulligan's

Licensed in 1782, Mulligan's (8 Poolbeg Street) is over 200 years old and is full of Victorian mahogany, well-worn counter tops and areas made snug with divides, screens and dark corners. There is lovely old lettering on the windows.

John F. Kennedy was a regular here in 1945 when he was working for the Hearst newspaper chain.

This gas-lit old pub has served James Joyce and Brendan Behan, and has become the congregating place for Dublin's journalists.

A sign in Mulligan's says:

Customers are allowed 30 minutes drinking-up time by which time they must have left the premises.

Neary's

Neary's (Chatham Street) is an Edwardian pub that has been frequented by actors for decades. Its back door, in Tangier Lane, is next to the stage door of the Gaiety Theatre. Two huge cast-iron arms protrude from the pub's facade, each holding a lantern. Brendan Behan drank here, as did Flann O'Brien who is rumoured to have written much of the novel *At Swim-Two-Birds* in one of Neary's quieter corners.

Flann O'Brien wrote:

When things go wrong and will not come right
Though you try the best you can.
When life looks black as the hour of night,
A pint of plain is your only man.

O'Donoghue's

At O'Donoghue's (Merrion Row) traditional Irish folk musicians gather to perform, with strings and whistles. Here, they will tell you, Senator Robert Kennedy sang along too during one Dublin visit.

Pollyhops

Pollyhops (Lucan Road) is a traditional Irish Pub in Newcastle. It dates back to 1847 and is steeped in tradition and folklore. Publican Polly used to supply the race tracks around Dublin with alcohol, taking this to the races on the back of her cart.

The Old Stand

The Old Stand (37 Exchequer Street) is an historical Dublin pub with strong sporting associations – with rugby, racing and golf. It lays claim to being one of the oldest public houses in Ireland!
One of the famous early drinkers at The Old Stand

was a poor cobbler called John Travere, renowned for his sharp wit and droll comments. When he closed his shoe stall on Hog Hill he continued his amusing comedy act to entertain the Old Stand patrons.

Formerly known as The Monico, The Old Stand was a favourite haunt of Michael Collins, who held informal meetings – and met his informers – here.

Toners

Toners (Lower Baggot), a pub that dates from 1817 was once a grocer's shop. Now its highly polished bar has multiple rows of small varnished drawers that once held sugar, tea, and other staple ingredients.

Toners pub claims to be the only one to have served a pint to William Butler Yeats, who preferred socializing at home in nearby Merrion Square. W. B. Yeats is reported to have told his friend, Gogarty, who brought him into the bar: *'I have seen a pub now. Will you kindly take me home?'*

The Palace Bar

The Palace Bar (21 Fleet Street) is a traditional, lively pub, once the favourite haunt of *The Irish*

Times staff. It was also very popular with Irish writers and poets living in Dublin in the early 1900s, including W. B. Yeats, Patrick Kavanagh and Flann O'Brien.

William Ryans

William Ryans (28 Parkgate Street)
This is a lovely Victorian pub full of snugs for private inbibing. This beautiful pub has an oval-shaped bar with fine ornate carpentry. Dark-stained flutings, arches and crowns all gleam with varnish.

A screen of stained glass runs behind the windows.

Secret snug patrons have included Gregory Peck Daniel Day-Lewis and Prince Albert of Monaco.

The private snugs at the rear of the William Ryans bar can be opened only when the barman releases a latch on the bar side of the snug's door so if customers want another drink or wish to leave, they have to summon attention with a bell.

Porterhouse

Porterhouse (16–18 Parliament Street, Temple Bar) sells Porterhouse offically honoured as, 'the best stout in the world 1998/1999' by the Brewing Industry Awards.

They also also brew eight
other beers.

Glimmerman

The Glimmerman in Stoneybatter
Michael Collins (who played a major part after the Uprising and helped bring about the treaty of 1921) is said to have hidden away weapons here.

An Irishman is the only man in the world who will step over the bodies of a dozen naked women to get to a bottle of stout.

Anonymous

Pub talk

When speaking about his drinking, Irish actor Richard Harris commented:

I often sit back and think, 'I wish I'd done that' and find out later that I already have.

Ireland is where strange tales begin
and happy endings are possible.
Charles Haughey

Talk of legends and fairy folk will often crop up when the Guinness flows and the Irish banter grows so, in order to hold your own in a Dublin pub, here's some inside information on the little people. . .

When I was growing up in Ireland between the wars, the supernatural was still a force, at least in the countryside. People might no longer really believe in leprechauns or banshees, but they would not have been greatly astonished to encounter them, and they certainly accepted that there were forces unknown to science, apparently directed by 'powers' capable of benevolent or malevolent actions.

Brian Inglis (*Natural and Supernatural - A History of the Paranormal*, 1992)

Leprechauns

The name leprechaun may have derived from the Irish words for shoemaker (leath bhrogan) or

Leprechauns are associated with music.

pygmy (luacharma'n). These old fellows, who are often intoxicated, are the guardians of ancient Viking treasure, buried in crocks or pots.

If caught, a leprechaun will promise great wealth in order to be allowed to go free but his magical coins either return to his purse or turn to leaves or ashes.

Stay sober and vigilant. If you take your eye off a leprechaun, he will immediately vanish.

The City of Dublin's St Patrick's Day Celebration includes the tradition of naming of a Grand Leprechaun. This honour is given to the person (or couple) who has made a significant contribution to the City of Dublin through volunteer efforts or leadership. The Grand Leprechaun leads the Saint Patrick's Day parade.

Cluricauns

A cluricaun is a kind of leprechaun who steals or borrows when night falls, raiding wine cellars and larders. Cluricauns will harness up and ride sheep, goats, dogs, geese and hens.

The early Celtic world had many horse cults that may have given rise to the notion of nightmare steeds such as . . .

Dullahans

Wild dullahans appear at midnight on certain Irish festivals or feast days. They are headless but hold a head in the saddle or in the right hand. The head, with its horrid grin, glows and may be held high, as a lantern to help the dullahan see into the distance.

Using a human spine as a whip, the dullahan rides a dark steed who snorts sparks and flames.

Anyone who watches him pass will have a basin of blood thrown in the face or be struck blind in one eye.

If the dullahan stops riding, a mortal dies.

Sometimes, country dullahans may drive black coaches drawn by six black horses, that set light to the bushes they pass. Locked gates fly open to let them through.

The Pooka

The pooka gets up to mischief at night and usually appears as a sleek, dark horse with sulphurous eyes and a long wild mane. The pooka tears down fences and gates, tramples crops and scatters livestock.

The pooka may also appear as a deformed goblin, a hairy, giant bogeyman, a black goat with curling horns, or a vast eagle.

Pookas will stop hens laying eggs or cows giving milk, and are known to swoop up late night travellers and throw them into muddy ditches or bogholes.

Changelings

Sometimes fairies will swap a stunted or deformed fairy offspring for a healthy mortal child. The bad-tempered changeling is always miserable; it howls and screeches all day long and drains good fortune from the house.

A changeling can be an actual fairy child, an old fairy disguised as a child or a 'stock' – an object, such as a piece of timber, that has assumed a child's form through magic.

Changelings are wizened little creatures with yellow skin like parchment and dark penetrating eyes. They often have a crooked back or a lame hand.

About two weeks after they arrive, changelings develop a full set of teeth. Their legs grow as thin as chicken bones and they have crooked hands like bird talons, covered with downy hair.

Changelings may be welcomed into an Irish pub because they are good at playing the fiddle and the Irish pipes.

Grogochs

Grogochs are half-human, half-fairy creatures who crossed to Ireland from Kintyre in Scotland. They look like tiny old men, covered in coarse, dense red hair and fur. Grogochs are really rather dirty. They wear just twigs and general muck gathered on their travels.

They will not enter a house if a priest or minister is inside . . . so if a grogoch is becoming a pain, inviting a clergyman into the house may serve to drive the nuisance away.

These grubby rascals live in caves or hollows and can make themselvs invisible when it suits them.

Grogochs will scuttle about the kitchen looking for odd jobs to do. They will help with planting, harvesting and domestic chores – in exchange for a jug of cream.

Banshees

These spirits warn members of ancient Irish families of imminent death. Tradition claims that a banshee can cry only for the O'Neills, O'Briens, O'Connors, O'Gradys and Kavanaghs.

The banshee can appear as a young woman, a stately matron or a raddled old hag. She may also appear as as the bean-nighe (a washerwoman), scrubbing the blood-stained clothes of whomsoever is about to die.

She usually wears either a grey, hooded cloak or a winding sheet or grave robe but the banshee may also appear as a hooded crow, stoat, hare, weasel or any animal associated with witchcraft.

The shamrock has been associated with good luck and making wishes come true ever since Saint Patrick used it to explain the Holy Trinity.

Banshees have been said to visit the great houses of Ireland and the courts of Irish kings. In 1437, King James I of Scotland was approached by a banshee in human form who foretold his murder.

Merrows

The word merrow or moruadh comes from the Irish *muir* (meaning sea) and *oigh* (meaning maid). Merrows are very beautiful and promiscuous.

Mermen are ugly and scaly, with long, pointed teeth and pig-like features. Perhaps, fortunately, they are rarely seen.

A merrow's feet are flat and a thin web joins her fingers. She has special clothing to enable her to travel through ocean currents and she may take on the appearance of a seal.

In order to come ashore, the merrow must abandon her cap or cloak, so any mortal who finds these and hides them has power over her; she cannot return to the sea until they are retrieved.

A fisherman who hides a merrow's cap or cloak may sometimes persuade the merrow to marry him. This may bring him great wealth as merrow brides often have fortunes of gold plundered from shipwrecks.

Merrow wives always have a fierce longing to return to the sea and will try to find their cloaks, even though this means that they must then desert their human husbands and children.

Some famous Irish families claim their descent from merrows, including the O'Flaherty and O'Sullivan families of Kerry and the MacNamaras of Clare.

Theatre and cinema

J. M. Synge

The Abbey Theatre

The Abbey Theatre was established by W. B. Yeats in 1904 and became the first state-subsidised theatre in the English-speaking world.

In 1907, early productions of J. M. Synge's *The Playboy of the Western World* at Abbey Theatre were deemed so shocking that they caused riots and the remainder of the play had to be acted out in dumbshow.

The original Abbey Theatre building was destroyed by fire on 18 July 1951.

The Gate Theatre

The Gate Theatre is housed in a sumptuous 18th-century building leased from the Rotunda Hospital.

Both Orson Welles and James Mason started their acting careers at The Gate.

The Point Theatre

The Point Theatre building was an old train depot. It was converted into a large international venue and opened in 1988.

Victorian theatres

The Gaiety Theatre – a splendid, tiered Victorian theatre – opened in 1871 and remains Dublin's longest-established, continuously-producing theatre.

The fine, old-fashioned Olympia Theatre – Dublin's first music hall – has a fading glory that makes it an ideal venue for international rock acts and stand-up comedians.

Bewley's Cafe Theatre

The elegant and intimate Bewley's Cafe Theatre is

a year-round venue for lunchtime drama.

Mahony Hall

The largest theatre in Dublin is the Mahony Hall in The Helix – the large, glass and granite Arts Centre at Dublin College University.

The Dublin Theatre Festival

This is one of the city's major annual events, presenting productions of new Irish plays and visiting international company productions.

Cinema-going

The cinema is extremely popular in Dublin – the Irish visit the cinema more often than any other Europeans.

Many movies feature Dublin

These include *The Commitments,*
In the Name of the Father
(filmed in Kilmainham Gaol),
Michael Collins and
Nora
(starring Ewan McGregor as James Joyce).

Section 481

When films are made in Ireland, the 'Section 481' tax code allows filmmakers to recoup 15 million Euros of their budgets.

Because of the generous tax breaks available to Hollywood filmmakers, Dublin doubled for New York in the 2002 film *In America,* and the script of *Rules of Attraction* was altered to feature Dublin instead of Los Angeles.

The Screen cinema

The Screen has some special seats for couples.

The Savoy cinema

The Savoy is Dublin city centre's oldest remaining cinema. One of its six screens is the largest in Ireland.

The Irish Film Institute

This is a national body dedicated to supporting Irish film heritage. It has an arthouse cinema in the Temple Bar quarter, showing independent and foreign-language films not shown at the multiplexes.

In 2001, the Irish Film Institute played a central role in establishing a travelling cinema or Cinemobile – a truck which transforms into a 100-seater state-of-the-art cinema.

Watching the travelling cinema machine transform from truck to Cinemobile is entertainment in itself!

Music

George Frederick Handel

The 18th century

George Frederick Handel lived in Abbey Street, Dublin in 1741–42.

Handel himself conducted the debut performance of *The Messiah* which took place at the Musick Hall in Fishamble Street, Dublin, on 13 April 1742.

Some of the biggest musical celebrations in Dublin were those held in Saint Patrick's Cathedral on Saint Cecilia's Day (the patron saint of music).

The 19th century

In the mid-19th century, evensong at Saint Patrick's Cathedral drew huge crowds and it was known as 'Paddy's Opera'.
Accounts describe the congregation standing under the noses of the singers and, after the anthem, stampeding out of the church.

Live music venues

Whelan's, one of Dublin's most prestigious live music venues, has had a public house on the site since 1772.

The Harcourt Hotel around St. Stephen's Green is one of the best venues for high-quality traditional-Irish music sessions.

The National Concert Hall in Earlsford Terrace is home to the National Symphony Orchestra and is the main venue for classical music and opera.

Large-scale rock concerts are sometimes held on Punchestown racecourse and at Croke Park and Lansdowne Road Stadiums.

The Green Energy Festival takes place at Dublin Castle (and other venues) every May and is headlined by many big-name rock and pop bands.

Rock and pop artists with Dublin roots

The rock band, Thin Lizzy, was formed in Dublin in 1969 by schoolfriends Phil Lynott and Brian Downey.

The Bob Geldof-fronted Boomtown Rats were formed in guitarist Garry Roberts' kitchen in Dublin in 1975.

U2 were formed in 1976 by seven pupils of Mount Temple Comprehensive School – including current members Bono, the Edge, Larry Mullen Jr. and Adam Clayton.

The Edge's real name is David Howell Evans (his parents are Welsh).

Bono's real name is Paul Hewson. The stage name comes from *Bono Vox* (roughly meaning 'good voice' in Latin), allegedly after a hearing aid company's advertising sign on the corner of Dame Street and South Great Georges Street in Dublin's city centre.

The pop singer and songwriter, Sinéad O'Connor, was born in Dublin and named after Sinéad de Valera, wife of Irish President Eamon de Valera and mother of the doctor presiding over the delivery.

The folk band, The Dubliners, were formed in Dublin and are named after the James Joyce novel of the same name.

The first four album covers for the Chieftains, the traditional folk band formed in Dublin, were designed by the famous sculptor, Edward Delaney.

Irish singer-songwiter, Damien Rice, was born in Kildare, near Dublin. He was able to record his hugely successful *O* album by exploiting a link with cousin David Arnold (the British composer best known for themes to *Independence Day*, recent James Bond films and *Little Britain*).

Ex-Westlife singer, Brian McFadden, was born in Artane, Dublin, on 12 April 1980.

Nicky Byrne, a member of the Irish pop band Westlife, was born in Dublin in 1978. He is married to Georgina, daughter of Irish Taoiseach (prime minister) Bertie Ahern.

Joking apart

The Irish gave the bagpipes to the Scots as a joke, but the Scots haven't seen the joke yet.

Oliver Herford, American Writer, 1863-1935

Statues and monuments

Several famous statues in Dublin have attracted fun 'alternative' names. Here follows a selection:

Anna Livia fountain

'The Floozie in the Jacuzzi' is the name given to this fountain formerly on O'Connell Street – now moved to Kilmainham. Personifying the river Liffey, Anna Livia was depicted as a woman sitting on a slope with water bubbing past her. It was also named 'The Hoor (meaning whore) in the Sewer' and 'Viagra Falls'.

Statue of Molly Malone

Molly Malone

Jeanne Rynhart's statue of Molly Malone in Grafton Street, showing her pushing her barrow of cockles and mussels, is known as: 'The Tart with the Cart'. The statue of the fictitious fishmonger with her ample cleavage is also known as 'The Dish with the Fish'.

James Joyce statue

On O'Connell Street and Earl Street North, this depicts the famous Irish writer walking with a cane in his hand. It is named 'The Prick with the Stick'.

Statue of James Joyce

The Millennium Spire

This 130-metre-high spire in O'Connell Street
has been variously dubbed:
'The Stiletto in the Ghetto'
'The Spike'
'The Scud in the Mud'
'The Nail in the Pale'
'The Metropole'
'The Stiffy by the Liffey'
'The Crank on the Bank'
'The Rod to God'
'The Pin in the Bin'
and
'The North Pole'.

Oscar Wilde

The painted statue of Oscar Wilde sitting on a boulder in Merrion Square has been called 'The Fag on the Crag' and 'The Quare in the Square'.

An Cailín Bán

On Sandymount Strand, close to the Martello Tower, stands An Cailín Bán – 'The Sore on the Shore'.

Thomas Moore

On a traffic island outside Trinity College, a statue of 1800s lyricist Thomas Moore shares its setting with a public toilet and has long been known as 'The Meeting of the Waters'.

The Millennium Clock

Erected to count down to the year 2000, this was set below the surface of the river. It had repeated problems with water ingress and time-keeping so it was removed, but not before it had been nick-named 'The Time (or the Chime) in the Slime'.

Women shoppers

A statue of two women (set by the Ha'penny Bridge) depicts them sitting on a bench chatting, with their shopping bags at their feet. It is called 'The Hags with the Bags'.

Statues destroyed or removed

Queen Victoria, unveiled outside Leinster House by Edward VII in 1904 (and called 'The Auld Bitch' by locals), was removed in 1947. It was left in storage before being given to the city of Sydney in Australia in the late 1980s.

The Lord Gough statue in Phoenix Park was blown up by Irish republicans in 1957.

King George II in St. Stephen's Green was blown up in 1937.

William of Orange in College Green was blown up 1946.

The Bowl of Light (thrown into the Liffey in 1953) was replaced with a flowerbed.

Nelson's Pillar in O'Connell Street was blown up in 1966.

The Washerwomen in Dame Street is undergoing redevelopment.

Equestrian statues have included:

William of Orange in College Green

King George II statue in St Stephen's Green.

No statues of people on horseback remain today as they have all been blown up by the IRA.

Nelson's Pillar, near the General Post Office in O'Connell Street, was blown up by the IRA in 1966 to mark the Easter Rising. Because only the top of the pillar was demolished, what remained until its removal was known as 'The Stump'.

Arthur Wellesley a.k.a. The Duke of Wellington

His was the only colonial monument that was not blown up or removed after the war of Independence. He defeated Napoleon and become Prime Minister of Britain.

O'Connell Street statues

Charles Stewart Parnell (north end of the street)
Daniel O'Connell (southern end)
The Dublin Martyrs, the 'Murdered Mayors'
Sir John Gray
Jim Larkin
Fr. Theobald Mathew

William Smith O'Brien

Cúchulainn (by the GPO)

Fr. Theobald Mathew

The Grand and Royal Canal statues include:

Patrick Kavanagh

Brendan Behan

St Stephen's Green statues include:

Fusiliers' Arch

William Coyningham

Wolfe Tone (blown up 1979 but since reconstructed)

Robert Emmet

The Lady Laura Grattan Font

Trinity College and College Green statues include:

William Lecky

George Salmon

Thomas Davis

Henry Grattan

Oliver Goldsmith

Edmund Burke

Thomas Moore

Phoenix Park statues include:

Wellington Monument

Phoenix Monument

Papal Cross

Other Dublin statues and monuments to note

Battle of the Custom House in Memorial Road
The Chariot of Life in Abbey Street
Children of Lir in Parnell Square
Dublin Yeomanry Memorial in Saint Andrew Street
Liberty Scaling the Heights in Grand Canal Street
The O'Connell Tower in the Prospect Cemetery
Padraig Sheahan Memorial in Hawkins Street
The 1974 Dublin and Monaghan
Bombings Memorial in Talbot Street

Politicians, leaders and other 'thinkers'

College Green has a statue of Henry Grattan who announced in the Grattan parliament of 1782 that, 'Ireland is now a nation.' Grattan was a leading politician in the old Irish Parliament.

A statue of patriot Thomas Davis (a nationalist leader in the 1960s) with its strange hands and odd-shaped body) has been named 'Frankenstein'.

On O'Connell Street, the trade unionist Jim Larkin is depicted, thowing his arms out wide. Larkin stated, 'The great appear great because you are on your knees – Arise!'

A statue of the political philosopher Edmund Burke stands outside the entrance gate of Trinity College from whence he graduated.

Temperance preacher, Matt Talbot, is yet another statue on O'Connell Street. His model, given her marching orders when drunk, destroyed the first version of this statue in an act of furious revenge.

The statue of Daniel O'Connell stands on the street named after him. The stout fellow is flanked by four Victories – one of whom sports a bullet hole in her nipple as a result of the 1916 hostilities.

Authors and artists

In Merrion Square, Oscar Wilde quotes adorn the pedestals of a male torso and a naked pregnant woman.

A statue of the playwright Oliver Goldsmith is set near the entrance gate of Trinity College which he once attended.

Turlough Carolan (1670-1738) is also remembered in St Patrick's Cathedral. He was a wandering harpist and poet, blinded by smallpox.

And others . . .

St Patrick's Cathedral has a statue of John McNeill Boyd, who valiantly tried to save the crew of the sinking Neptune in 1861 but died in the attempt.

The *Tree of Gold* structure by Eamonn O'Doherty outside the Central Bank near Trinity College depicts groups of skate kids loafing about.

Near Custom House is a 1990s memorial to the Great Famine victims of 1845–47, sculpted by Rowan Gillespie and depicting the starving, desperate Irish people.

On City Quay, the Merchant Seamen Memorial by Sir John Rogerson's Quay remembers the Irish merchant ships and the sailors that lost their lives in World War Two.

A few rather odd statues include:

A Cow in Jervis Street
A Cinema Usher in Hawkins Street
A Headless Saint, Gardiner Street
The Strong Striking Bear at IFSC
Two Children in Portland Row

Parks and gardens

Dublin has more than 1,000 acres of parkland, with 35 developed parks.

Phoenix Park

At 1,752 acres, Phoenix Park is the largest city park in Europe, more than twice the size of New York's Central Park.

Phoenix Park is home to the official residence of the President of Ireland.

Dublin Zoo in Phoenix Park bred the first ever lions in captivity in 1857.

Dublin Zoo raised Caibre, the lion who roars in the opening sequence of MGM films.

Phoenix Park's Ashtown Castle, a medieval tower house, used to be incorporated into an 18th-century mansion and was only 'rediscovered' when the mansion was demolished due to dry rot.

A herd of fallow deer roam in Phoenix Park.

Blessington Street Basin

This tranquil inner-city haven for visitors and wildlife is dubbed 'Dublin's secret garden' as it remains largely undiscovered by thousands of passing people.

Saint Stephen's Green

As well as containing statues, fine horticulture and floral displays, this public park – Dublin's best preserved Georgian Square – contains a fine collection of the old Dublin city lamp posts.

In 1930, Merrion Square Park was purchased from the Pembroke Estate by the Roman Catholic Church as a site for a cathedral but the project never materialised.

Ireland's best known Victorian public park, Saint Stephen's Green, was originally enclosed in 1664.

Until 1800, St. Stephen's Green was a common ground used for public hangings and whippings.

In summer, free concerts are held here in the bandstand.

The National Botanic Gardens

This contain about 20,000 plant species and cultivars.

Fitzwilliam Square

The residents of the elegant Georgian square still hold keys to the central garden.

Gardens of remembrance

The Garden of Remembrance marks the spot where several leaders of the 1916 Easter Rising were held before being taken to Kilmainham Gaol.

The War Memorial Gardens are dedicated to the 49,400 Irish soldiers who died in World War I – all the names are contained in the granite bookrooms.

Croke Park

The Gaelic Athletics Association (Gaelic football and hurling) owns the famous Croke Park stadium and forbids the playing in the stadium of 'foreign games' such as soccer or rugby.

The largest ever attendance at Croke Park was 90,556 in 1961, when Down played Offaly in the All Ireland Gaelic Football Final.

Landsdowne Road

This stadium held its first rugby international in 1878, when Ireland played England.

The highest attendance at a soccer match in Lansdowne Road was 53,500 to see Ireland play France in a World Cup qualifier in 1981.

Bridges, water and trade

Dublin rivers

The main rivers of Dublin are the Liffey, Poddle, Dodder and Tolka.

The River Liffey

This rises near Kippure, a mountain in County Wicklow, and flows for 75 miles (125 km) before entering the Irish sea in Dublin Bay.

Liffey bridges

The Liffey is spanned by the following bridges in Dublin: West-Link Bridge; Sean Heuston Bridge; Frank Sherwin Bridge; Roy O'More Bridge; James Joyce Bridge; Mellowes Bridge; Fr. Mathew Bridge; O'Donovan Rossa Bridge; Grattan Bridge; Ha'penny Bridge (pedestrian only); Millennium footbridge (pedestrian only); O'Connell Bridge; Butt Bridge; Talbot Memorial Bridge; Sean O'Casey Bridge (pedestrian only); East-Link Bridge.

Ha'penny Bridge

Officially named Wellington Bridge, this is the old pedestrian bridge linking Temple Bar to the north bank of the Liffey. It acquired its unofficial name from the toll paid to cross the river – one old half penny.

O'Connell Bridge

Originally, a rope bridge on this site carried only one man and a donkey at a time. A humped, symmetrical granite bridge (named Carlisle Bridge) was built here between 1791 and 1794.

In 1879–82, Carlisle Bridge was widened to improve the streetscape and relieve traffic congestion. It was renamed after Daniel O'Connell and it is now unique in Europe as the only traffic bridge as wide as it is long.

The canals

The building of the Grand Canal began in 1756 and it reached the river Shannon by 1803.

The main line is 82 miles (131 km) with 43 locks, 5 of which are double locks. The Barrow line is 28 miles (43 km) long with 9 locks including 2 doubles.

The Royal Canal, begun in 1790, runs through the north of the city. A true Dubliner or 'Jackeen' is said to have been born between the Grand Canal and the Royal Canal.

In December 1792, 150 people (many of them drunk) forced their way onto a barge leaving Dublin for Athy, in spite of warnings from the captain. The boat capsized and 5 men, 4 women and 2 children drowned.

Port of Dublin

The original Port of Dublin was situated upriver at Wood Quay, close to Christchurch Cathedral.

In medieval times Dublin shipped cattle hides to Britain and the continent, and the returning ships carried wine, pottery and other goods.

Until the early 1700s, Dublin Bay in its natural state was wild, open and exposed to every wind. Ships could sometimes not reach the city for several weeks at a time and shipwrecks were common.

To protect the south side of the harbour, the South Bull Wall was constructed in 1753 – bull is another word for strand, and the strands either side of the mouth of the Liffey were known as the North and South Bulls.

The North Bull Wall was built at the recommendation of a survey in 1800 by Captain William Bligh, famous for his role in the mutiny on the Bounty.

In the 1700s, Dublin prospered as merchants shipped cargos of linen and farm produce to Britain and farther afield. Returning ships carried coal and the luxury goods that were in demand in the great Georgian Houses.

To save time, ship passengers and packets of mail used to land at the end of the Bull Wall to be rowed to the city in smaller boats.

Trade

Dublin is Ireland's largest port and major exporter.

Dublin is the largest manufacturing city in Ireland, with mainly light manufacturing enterprises.

Transport and roads

Buses

Bus Átha Cliath (Dublin Bus) operates nearly 200 daytime routes and 24 night services.

Dublin daytime buses usually start running at about 6am and the last city-centre buses leave town about 11.30pm.

Bus fares are payable in coins and only the exact fare is acceptable – passengers who overpay are issued with ‘change tickets’ which have to be presented at the Dublin Bus office to be converted to cash.

A notorious Dublin character used to jump onto the old buses and pretend to shoot the terrified passengers, shouting, 'Bang! Bang!' He had to take early retirement with the arrival of automatic bus doors.

DART

The Dublin Area Rapid Transit (DART) system is the only electrified railway in the country, following the east coast.

The DART service that runs from Dalkey to Killiney has amazing views of Dublin Bay.

Luas

Luas (Irish for 'speed') is a light-rail or tram system consisting of two currently-unconnected lines.

The sleek, silver Luas trams reach a top speed of 70 km/h on off-road sections, but travel at lower speeds near vehicles and pedestrians.

Air travel

Dublin and Shannon are the only two European airports with U.S. border preclearance facilities.

The first flight from Dublin Airport was on January 19 1940, to Liverpool, England.

Dublin Airport's original terminal building, built in 1941, was modelled on the bridge of a luxury liner and won an architectural award.

The Dublin–London air route is the busiest in the EU and second-busiest in the world with over 4.4 million passengers per year.

The railways

The Dublin and Kingstown Railway, opened in 1834, was the first railway built in Ireland and one of the earliest dedicated commuter railways in the world.

The unusual track gauge of Ireland's mainline railways (1600 mm, 5 ft 3 in) is otherwise found only in Brazil and the Australian states of Victoria and South Australia.

Heuston Station, the main railway station for the south and west of the republic, was named after Sean Heuston, an Easter Rising rebel who worked in the station offices.

Connolly Station, which mainly serves the Sligo and Dublin-Belfast routes, was named after patriot James Connolly on the 50th anniversary of the Easter Rising.

Roads and streets

In the 1700s, the Wide Streets Commission oversaw the drastic reshaping of Dublin by demolishing or widening old medieval streets and creating large Georgian thoroughfares.

Ceremonial travel

The Irish Cavalry Corps (which provides presidential escorts) use Japanese motorbikes for ceremonies, while Britain, France (and most other states that use horses in ceremonies) prefer to use Irish horses!

The Vikings

A Viking attack

Early days

The Vikings first established a base at the mouth of the River Liffey in CE 841. This was used as trading and pirate base until CE 902 when it was destroyed by native Irish.

The Vikings returned in about CE 917 and established an enclosed town on high ground beside where the river Poddle entered the Liffey.

Trade

At the end of the 10th century, Dublin was the most important Norse port in the West and one of Europe's leading slave and trading centres.

Viking ships left Dublin bound for the Isle of Man, Chester, Bristol, Scotland, the Hebrides, and the Mediterranean Sea.

Ships arriving at Dublin carried wine and ceramics from England, soapstone from Shetland, silks from Baghdad, glass bracelet stones from Germany, tin from Cornwall, silver from the Middle East and walrus tusks from the Arctic.

Slaves, mainly Britons and Picts, were important in building and maintaining Viking Dublin.

The successful trading town founded by the Vikings flourished until the late 12th century, when the city was attacked and conquered by an Anglo-Norman force.

Streets and houses in Viking Dublin

Viking Dublin was a network of ordered streets, pathways and houses, with plots and yards divided from each other by low post-and-wattle fences.

The town was first surrounded by an earth bank topped by a post-and-wattle palisade. About CE 1000, a town wall of stone was built.

The streets of the Viking Dublin were surfaced with gravel and stones, wattle mats or split logs.

Craftsmen of the same type were sited close together in certain areas of the town: leather workers were in today's High Street area, amber jewellers and wood workers in Fishamble Street, and fishermen, boat builders and merchants were along the waterfront.

A typical Dublin Viking house was 6m x 5m. A thatch roof was supported by 4 posts inside. The post-and-wattle walls were a metre high, with a door in each gable but no windows. The fire was in a centre aisle and a hole in the roof let out the smoke.

Either side of the centre aisle was a raised bedding area of brushwood topped with straw or grass. These beds were used as seats during the day.

A Dublin Viking house lasted about 15 years. After this, the roof – usually made of barley straw attached to a layer of turf on a mesh of wattles – began to sag and leak.

Dress

Dublin Viking men wore trousers, a shirt and a simple brightly-coloured tunic over all. They also wore woollen cloaks, furs, hides and even silk caps and neckerchiefs.

Dublin Viking women wore a linen or woollen chemise under a woollen dress suspended from a pair of shoulder straps. A shawl or cloak was worn outside, fastened at the neck with a brooch.

Dublin Viking men and women wore low, flat shoes laced with thongs. They also wore belts which held knives, purses and combs.

Dublin Vikings prized silver and jewellers made armlets and brooches from it. The native Irish ringed-pin became popular among the Vikings and these have been found at all great Viking centres abroad including Newfoundland.

Excavations

Major excavations carried out between 1962 and 1981 yielded huge quantities of Viking artifacts, now on show at The National Museum Annexe.

The excavations were never completed and the corporation of Dublin built two enormous Civic Offices on the site!

The dark side of Dublin

Well, there's no one at all, they do be saying,
but is deserving of some punishment
from the very minute of his birth.
Lady Isabella Augusta Gregory 1852-1932

The Battle of Clontarf

In 1014 Brian Boru, High King of Ireland, decisively defeated the Vikings at the Battle of Clontarf near Dublin, but was murdered in his tent by some allies of the Vikings.

Of the 7–8,000 Vikings and allied forces, about 6,000 were killed, including almost all the leaders.

Irish losses at the Battle of Clontarf were between 1,600 and 4,000, including their king and most of his sons.

Starvation

In 1295, food shortages in Dublin were so bad that the poor were driven to eat the criminals on the gallows.

Getting hooked

In the 1700s a gang of Liberty Boy tailors left their Ormond Boy butcher rivals hanging by their jaws from their own meat hooks.

Going for the jugular

When Wolfe Tone slit his throat in jail in 1798, he cut his windpipe instead of the jugular vein. He had to endure eight days of agony before he died but his last words were reputed to be, *'I find I am but a bad anatomist.'*

Spine chiller

Bram Stoker, author of Dracula, lived in Kildare Street, Dublin. *The Dracula Experience* in Clontarf Road offers a spine-chilling experience with exhibits on Transylvania, Dracula's Castle, the Blood Laboratory and Dracula's Lair.

Wolfe Tone

Not invincible

In Phoenix Park on 6 May 1882, Lord Cavendish (chief secretary of Ireland and nephew of British Prime Minister Gladstone) and his under-secretary Thomas Burke were stabbed to death by members of a Fenian splinter group called the Invincibles.

Death tolls

On 22 November 1920, in response to the assassination of 14 British Intelligence officers, British troops fired machine guns into a crowd watching a Gaelic football game at Croke Park stadium, killing 14 and injuring 65 people.

In 1922, under emergency legislation during the Civil War, 13,000 people were incarcerated for over 7 months, 77 were executed and the death toll from imprisonment and hunger strikes was 264.

The Dublin Hellfire Club

This 1700s hunting lodge was the venue for the Hellfire Club who held satanic rituals and made animal and human sacrifices.

There are reports of srange dark figures and shadows inside and out of the former club.

It is said that when the Dublin Hellfire Club was active, any people who arrived uninvited were unlikely to survive the night – or became semi-zombies thereafter.

To counteract the vile vibes, a priest blessed the building in the early 1800s and an exorcist was brought in to help in the late 1800s.

Horrors here included the setting on fire of a woman stuffed inside a barrel, plus the ritual beating and murder of a poor deformed boy.

At a meeting of the club in 1740, a servant is said to have spilt a drink on one Thomas Whaley, who was so enraged that he had the servant doused in brandy and set ablaze. The subsequent fire burnt down the building and killed several members of the club.

St. Michan's Church

In 1095, St Michan, probably a Danish Bishop, built the first church here on the site of an ancient oak forest. In the dark crypt below, coffins are stacked in untidy piles with arms, legs and heads protruding.

Although dead for over 500 years, the bodies in the vault of St Michan's Church have been preserved like mummies but with joints supple enough to move. This may possibly be due to chemical changes in the air caused by the remains of the oak forest.

Explorers of the macabre crypt here have heard strange voices and whispers and felt ice cold fingers run down their necks.

Kilmainham Gaol

Here the leaders of the 1916 uprising were detained and many were also executed here in May 1916. The last to die was James Connolly who had to be tied into a chair first, as he was unable to stand on his own due to his severe injuries that included a broken ankle.

During its restoration in the 1960s, a caretaker saw that the chapel lights, which he had just turned off, had been switched back on again. He went across to switch them off and returned home but the chapel lights were on once again. He made the long walk to the chapel three times that night.

During the restoration of the gaol, a man painting the dungeons was blown hard against a wall and had to fight hard to escape from this strange force. He refused ever to work in, or even visit, the gaol again.

Another volunteer was decorating the '1916 Corridor' when he heard what he took to be a colleague's heavy footsteps, climbing the stone stairs and walking along the passage behind him but no one else was there. The footsteps continued and 'walked' right past him.

One guide has claimed that there is an evil aura around the balcony of the chapel. Others sense the gaol to be a tranquil place and speak of how the eyes of the thousands of past inmates watch them - but not in an unfriendly way.

Malahide Castle

This 1185 fortress is set north of Dublin. Here a 16th-century Flemish carving above a fireplace mysteriously disappeared when Oliver Cromwell invaded and gave the fortress to Miles Corbet. After the Restoration of Charles II in 1660, and the execution of Corbet, the Castle was restored to the Talbot family – and the carving reappeared!

A ghost called Puck returns here regularly. He is believed to be a 1400s watchman who, having imbibed liberally, fell asleep at his post as an enemy stormed the Castle. In remorse, he hanged himself from the minstrel's gallery.

Puck's spirit reappears whenever he disagrees with any changes. In 1975, when an auctioneer was compiling an inventory of the castle's fixtures and fittings, he saw the unmistakable figure of Puck shaking his head in disapproval.

Killakee House

In 1968 the O'Brien's bought a derelict building intending to turn it into an arts centre. The workmen soon grew used to eerie sounds and uncanny happenings – and the sudden appearance and disappearance of a large black cat.

Mrs O'Brien soon saw the creature too, squatting on the flagstones of the hallway and glaring. Every door was locked both before and after its sudden appearances and disappearances.

In March 1968, a painter and two other men were working at Killakee House, when the temperature dropped alarmingly, a door swung wide open and there was a low, angry growl. A hideous black cat with blazing red eyes was snarling there. Following this, Margaret O'Brien had the building exorcised and things quietened down.

In October 1969, a group of actors staying at the arts centre there held a séance and the disturbances began again. Two nuns would appear in the gallery. A local medium claimed that the phantoms were the unhappy spirits of two women who had assisted at satanic rituals at the notorious Hell Fire Club in the 1700s (see page 402).

Local legend tells the society had revelled in debauched rituals including the worshipping of cats as a representative of Satan himself and the burning alive of a black cat on at least one occasion.

In July 1970, a dwarfish skeleton was discovered buried beneath the kitchen floor of the building. Also in the grave was the brass statuette of a demon. A priest gave the body a proper burial and the manifestations stopped.

Today, Tom McAssey's portrait of The Black Cat of Killakee gazes down from one of the walls with its eerie red eyes.

St Kevin's Graveyard

In the 1800s, this place was notorious as the haunt of body snatchers for Dublin surgeons who needed fresh bodies.

Intrigued by its reputation as a haunted graveyard, one recent photographer took shots in total darkness. When the films were developed, several sreange glowing orbs, some with motion trails below them, appeared where nothing had been visible to
the naked eye.

National Wax Museum

For a dip into the dark side of Dublin, here there is a Chamber of Horrors and exhibits such as Red Riding Hood's bad wolf, goblins, a dismembered giant and Vlad the Impaler – plus rattling chains and horrific screams.

Final thought

The city has seen cruelty, poverty and starvation but, however dark these might be, the bubbling personalities and wit of the Dubliners, the Guinness, blue skies behind stunning buildings, soft rain and Irish music will soon restore the spirits.

The President's official residence in Phoenix Park was built 1751–54

GENERAL DISCLAIMER